Attitudes Are
Contagious

Are Yours Worth Catching?

Attitudes Are Contagious

Are Yours Worth Catching?

Dennis E. Mannering with
Wendy K. Mannering

OPTIONS UNLIMITED, INC.
Green Bay Wisconsin

Published by OPTIONS UNLIMITED, INC.
617 Sunrise Lane
Green Bay, WI 54301

Publisher's Cataloging-in-Publication Data
Mannering, Dennis E.
      Attitudes are contagious–are yours worth catching? / Dennis E.
      with Wendy K. Mannering -- Green Bay, WI : Options Unlimited,
      Inc., 2000.
          p.   cm.
      ISBN 0-945890-00-1

      1. Employee motivation.   I. Mannering, Wendy K.   II. Title.
HF5549.5.M63 M36   2000   99-64005
658.31'4   dc—21   CIP

PROJECT COORDINATION BY JENKINS GROUP, INC.

03 02 01 00 ✱ 5 4 3 2

Printed in the United States of America

To those who allow for our fullest motivation:
Dennis Jr., Brian, and Bob,
Austin, Alyssa, Katie, Vanessa and Brock.
May your lives be as richly blessed
as you have blessed ours.

CONTENTS

	Foreword	*9*
	Preface	*11*
	Introduction	*13*

CHAPTER 1   MOTIVATION IS AN ATTITUDE   15
Defining the Problem
Motivation vs. Movement
Four Statements on Motivation
The Unquenchable Thirst
What is Motivation?

CHAPTER 2   ATTITUDES ARE CONTAGIOUS...
ARE YOURS WORTH CATCHING?   25
Attitudes vs. Facts
It's the Little Things that Make
the Big Difference
Look for the Positive
Act — Feel — Think!

CHAPTER 3   YOU ARE WORTH MILLIONS   37
Defining Self-esteem
The Cause of Low Self-esteem
The Solution
You are Worth Millions!
Caring for Our "Millions"

CHAPTER 4   GO WITH GOALS AND HIT
YOUR TARGET   47
Goals vs Pipe Dreams
Research on the Value of Goal Setting

CONTENTS

Why Don't We?
The How-to's of Goal Setting
Think Big
Mapping Your life's Journey
Do It Now!
The Three V's of Goal Setting

CHAPTER 5   YOU'VE GOT A PROBLEM —
THAT'S TERRIFIC!   63
Getting a Perspective
Problems vs. Opportunities
The Measure of Our Worth
People Problems
A Problem-Solving System

CHAPTER 6   BELIEVE AND ACHIEVE   75
The Key to Motivation
Components of Belief
Belief Leads to Achievement
Believe More in Your Work
Avoid "Dream Killers"

CHAPTER 7   LIFE IS TERRIFIC — GET WITH IT!   85
A Critical Attitude for Motivation
The Benefits of Enthusiasm
Begin with a Smile
The Value of a Smile

Epilogue   *95*
Postscript   *99*
About the Author   *100*
Comments Welcome   *103*
Order Information   *104*

FOREWORD

*I*T WAS 1989 WHEN I WAS DOING MARKETING FOR A training company that I heard about Dennis Mannering's book. I called Dennis and said that we might be interested in selling his book at our programs. Dennis sent me a copy to read and said that if I liked it, maybe we could work something out.

Now at that time, I was reading at least one book a month on motivation, several articles a week of a motivational nature and constantly listening to tapes by some of the "grand masters of motivation." I received Dennis' *Attitudes* book in the morning mail and immediately read the first chapter. I read more over lunch and finished the book that night. I could not go to sleep! That night I made the decision. I mapped out a plan to leave the business I was with to start my own company. This book moved me to change my circumstances.

I have always possessed a positive attitude and enthusiasm toward most things in life. Deep down I think I knew that "attitudes are contagious," even though I didn't consciously think about it. After I read this book, I realized we all have an influence on others: good, bad, right, wrong or indifferent. We have a choice to influence others in a positive way or not!

Over the years, I have become good friends with Dennis and his wife, Wendy. They have "contagious attitudes" about their family, their business, the speaking profession and life as a whole. They "walk the talk."

Since reading this book it has been my goal to be "contagious in a positive way with everyone I come in contact with." In every presentation I make, I tell my story about the impact this book has had on me.

This book should be required reading for kids, families, training departments, corporations and associations. Anyone owning a business or going into business could benefit themselves and their customers by reading this book. When you are finished with this book, **don't put it away on the bookshelf. Pass it on! Share it with others. Buy one for those you care about.** Most importantly, have an attitude that is "worth catching!"

Jeff Staads
Business Resource Center

PREFACE

*T*HIS BOOK HAS BEEN A LABOR OF LOVE. IT IS NOT intended as "the final word" on motivation and success, but rather as the authors' public statement gleaned from years of reading, observation and personal experience.

Perhaps there is nothing new to say on motivation, only original ways of saying it. There are so many individuals I am indebted to for their insights on motivation.

Much of my inspiration to pursue the areas of success, motivation and positive attitudes started with early acquisition of recordings by the late Cavett Robert and the late Earl Nightingale. Writings by Dale Carnegie, Herzberg, Maslow, Blake and Mouton, William James and various authors of the Bible were real "motivators" to me.

In recent years, I have spent hundreds of hours acquainting myself with the works of Norman Vincent Peale, Robert Schuller, Zig Ziglar, and Bob Conklin.

There are countless individuals who have personally encouraged me and supported the efforts involved in bringing this book to fruition. Thanks go to Linda Morrison, who typed rough drafts and final drafts for my first edition over and over again.

Thanks to Lisa Koltz for committing my book to disc so that work could be done for the second edition.

Thanks also to my associates Jack Schleisman, Jim Morrison and Paul Harrison for their constant support. But most of all, thank you to my wife, Wendy, for countless hours spent persuading, prodding and actually putting the words that I had said on paper for me. She has also added her own ideas and input to the second edition of this book making it a true joint venture. Her total commitment to this project was invaluable.

INTRODUCTION

When the original manuscript for this book was written in 1986, I had no idea the response would be so positive. At times it has been overwhelming.

Over the last twelve years, I've heard from dozens of people who have shared with me the impact this little book has had on their lives. One man wrote, "I never realized that I already possessed everything I needed in order to change my life...for the better. Thank you."

Years after the book was written a lady came up to me after a speaking engagement and said, "I keep your book on my nightstand and read it every week. I've had it seven years and it's getting pretty worn. Please send me a new one."

Perhaps what pleases me most are the number of young people who have read this book over the years. Several high schools have used the book as a resource text for a human relations unit in marketing and business or as a general interest book in other classes. The opportunity to impact young adults in high school and college is indeed a joy to me, since I spent over ten years as an educator before entering the speaking and training profession.

The importance of attitude continues to be researched and validated. The development of positive attitudes is encouraged whether in our personal or professional lives. As we enter the information age and leave the knowledge age, technology education is exploding. With this explosion of technology, the need for developing positive attitudes, human relation skills and good interpersonal relationships will be greater than ever. Whether I am educating a sales group, talking about customer service or working with managers to help them motivate people to peak performance, attitude plays a key role.

The chapter on goal setting has impacted people more than any other segment of the book with the exception of the Epilogue. If you want to change your life for the better, the chapter on goal setting will help you do that. It is written simply and is easy to understand. The idea is to get you started and then you can do much more with the concept.

The Epilogue of the book has been featured in two *Chicken Soup for the Soul* books, as well as an Asian Pacific Journal. It is my most requested signature story when speaking. (Now, don't skip to the Epilogue first!)

The chapters are sequenced the way they are for a reason. I really believe that the first attitude one has to work on is self-esteem - a positive attitude about one's self. Without that you can't do much with the others.

Thirteen years have passed. So, after ten printings with the same format, it is time for an update. Though none of the information in the original book is changed, some updating of stories, illustrations and facts has taken place.

Chapter 1

MOTIVATION IS AN ATTITUDE

OTIVATION IS A VERY POPULAR TOPIC THESE DAYS. When our company is called by an organization to provide training, so often the topic we're asked to address is "motivation." Our first question is usually, "How many people do you have working for you?" The typical response is very close to, "Oh, about half of them," or "Well, Joe's been working ever since we threatened to fire him." The sad truth is that many people quit looking for work the minute they find a job!

Why is this? What has happened to the work ethic in America? With almost zero unemployment and changing attitudes about work versus leisure time, finding and keeping truly motivated employees has become most companies' greatest challenge.

When we talk to the youth of today and ask them to use five descriptive words for the word work, they use words like *hard, boring, dull, dirty* or *tedious.* Where do these impressions come from? Why are the words *challenging, rewarding, fulfilling, purposeful* or *beneficial* missing from adjectives used by youth that face a lifetime in the world of work? What are their role models telling them?

One explanation may be that many parents subject their children to listening to their complaints about their work. One teenager I was interviewing observed, "I get home from school before either Mom or Dad. Then Mom gets home and warns me not to talk to her for awhile because she has had a bad day at work because of her "awful" boss or someone at work who "makes her sick." Then Dad gets home. And if you think Mom has a terrible job, you should hear Dad! He is even worse. Sometimes he and Mom actually get into an argument over who has the worst job and, believe it or not, they both want to win the argument!"

Is it any wonder that many young people today dread the prospect of going to work, and once they get there they are not highly motivated in their jobs?

I am not really pointing fingers, but I am searching for the reason why so many workers today are not motivated by the work they do and, instead, provide the type of role model just described by this teenager.

Maybe something is missing in the work environment. Perhaps their own personal perceptions regarding the lack of importance of what they do has led to this dissatisfaction. It is possible that too many are waiting for their bosses to do something to motivate them to work.

The bottom line is, there are great misconceptions about what true motivation is, and when there is a shortage of it, fingers get pointed in all directions, except at our own selves.

There are numerous ideas on what motivates people. Labor unions would have us believe high wages and fringe benefits will do the trick. Employers would love to believe their workers really want to help them make a big profit. Every once in awhile, a company gives its workers a raise or a new fringe benefit, and everyone is happy...for awhile. But in a matter of time, the same problems arise. Discontent returns. Motivated people become harder and harder to find. Why?

MOTIVATION VS. MOVEMENT

I believe there are several reasons. One is that many employers really don't want motivated workers. They confuse the word *motivation* with the word *movement*. They want people who do what they want when they want and how they want it done. A motivated person may not necessarily do just that. He may be looking for new and better ways to do things. He may rock the boat by suggesting innovative ideas for a company content to do things the way they have always been done. So the motivated employee may find his ideas squelched and, along with his ideas, his motivation.

To further illustrate the difference between motivation and movement, I like to use the example of the little dog I used to have when I was a boy.

Every morning he would lie in front of our gate to wait for his last bit of attention before I left for school. Now, there were two ways I could get him to move, so that I could get through the gate. I could firmly plant my foot in the center of his behind and he would move. Or, I could call the dog and he would come running because he loves me and wouldn't want to do anything to make me late for school (and he knows I may just have a treat for him in my pocket). In the first method, the dog moved because I wanted him to move. That is **movement.** With the second method, he moved because he wanted to move. That's **motivation.** He had an inner directed desire to move...for his reasons, not mine.

FOUR STATEMENTS ON MOTIVATION

But there is more to understanding motivation. Through research, studying under people like Bob Conklin, and simply observing people, I have learned and discovered some basic principles about human motivation.

Number one, **you can't motivate other people**. As you can see from the examples I have used, you may move people, but you can't motivate them. That's got to be an inside job. What you **can** do is create an environment in which an individual will be positively motivated. I'll explain more on this point later.

Second, and you may find this hard to believe, all people are already motivated. The catch is, it's not necessarily positive motivation. That student or worker who is habitually late for school or work is motivated to sleep late or, perhaps, to party too late into the night. The salesman who spends more time in the coffee shop than out with his clients is motivated to socialize, relax or protect his ego from rejection rather than work and earn money.

Third, and one of the hardest principles of motivation to understand, is that people do things **for their reasons and not your reasons**. In other words, trying to convince or motivate someone to do something by showing them how you will benefit is futile. You would be much more effective by recognizing the needs of the individual and showing them how they stand to benefit. To tell a worker that it will benefit you, the supervisor, will not motivate the worker. But if you can illustrate to the worker that a certain action will make the job more interesting for him, or more lucrative, there's motivation. He'll be doing something because he wants to do it. The tricky part is figuring out what each person really wants, what their hot buttons are. Each person you interact with will have different desires and values that will determine the things that will truly inspire and motivate them.

The ability to recognize individual needs is a skill that must be developed to apply the fourth basic statement on motivation, as well. That statement (admittedly said in many ways before) is this: **If you treat all people the same, you are mistreating most of the people.** "Now wait a minute," some might respond. Is that what you're saying? You probably pride yourself on being fair with your employees, your students, or your children by dealing with each one in exactly the same way. I would, in turn, ask this question. Did you find that the effectiveness of your "fair treatment" was equal in each situation, or were you more successful with one individual than another?

I am assuming the answer to the second part of that question is yes, simply because I have found that no two individuals respond to the same stimuli or treatment in the same way. Why? Every person has different needs for every facet of his or her life, from job challenges to recognition to social needs.

Vince Lombardi was a master at recognizing individual needs. One story told about him involves Paul Hornung and Jerry Kramer. Lombardi knew that what motivated Paul to play his heart out for the Green Bay Packers was different from what motivated Jerry.

Paul Hornung was a player with average talent in several positions on the field. Lombardi recognized this, decided to make Hornung "Mr. Versatile," and proceeded to convince Hornung he was just that... "Mr. Versatile." Lombardi would put his arm around Paul and say, "Paul, you're the greatest. Now get out there and show the crowd how terrific you are." And Hornung did.

On the other hand, Jerry Kramer was a man blessed with a great deal of talent, but he was just a little on the lazy side. Lombardi recognized both traits and knew just what he had to do. When Kramer would come off the field and say, "How'd I do, Coach?" Lombardi would hold his nose and say, "You stunk up the field! Now get back out there and get to work!" Along with those seething words often came a swift kick in Kramer's behind. How did Kramer respond? He went out there and performed even better than before.

Years later, when asked why he didn't kick Hornung like he kicked Kramer, Lombardi roared, "Because he probably would have kicked me back!" Whether this part of the story is exaggerated is not really of importance to me. What Lombardi was really saying was that he knew each player responded to a different type of recognition and reward, and he was willing to do what he had to do to meet those individual needs. Did this philosophy work for him? I believe his record of success speaks for itself.

THE UNQUENCHABLE THIRST

There was another fellow by the name of Abraham Maslow, a noted psychologist, who studied the nature of man in depth and developed the theory that all human beings follow a sort of step-by-step progression of needs as they go through life. As our needs are met, according to Maslow, we move up the ladder to the next level of need that motivates us to work and strive to attain satisfaction. I believe his theory helps us to understand those needs that motivate people and it also helps employers and supervisors practice appropriate motivational techniques with each individual. To illustrate Maslow's "Hierarchy of Needs," I'd like to use the story of Charlie, a poor soul who is out of work, tired, cold and hungry. This illustration takes place at the turn of the 20th century, when there was no such thing as welfare, so Charlie is desperately seeking employment.

Picture Charlie walking along a dirt road. He comes upon a sign that simply states, "Ditch Diggers Wanted - Apply Within." Being hungry and tired, he rushes into the office and eagerly asks the manager for a job. The manager replies, "Well, Charlie, we don't pay much in wages here, but see those uniforms over there? We'll provide you with five of those woolen shirts and five pairs of woolen pants plus two pairs of warm boots. Also, my wife is a terrific cook and we'll provide you with three warm meals each day. And out behind our house are the workers' barracks. You can sleep there free of charge."

Needless to say, Charlie took the job and for the first time in weeks he was warm, full of good food and had a good night's rest. His physical needs were met. And was he motivated? You bet! He dug ditches like ditches had never been dug before...for two weeks. Then, one day, the manager came by and saw Charlie leaning on his shovel.

"What's wrong, Charlie? Why aren't you working?" the manager asked.

"Well, boss, you know that one night off you give us? Well, I went down to the local tavern and I was talking with some guys from the ABC Ditch Digging Company. And you know, they've got Blue Cross/Blue Shield. We don't have that. What if I drop a shovel on my toe? Who's going to pay for that? And they have a retirement plan. I mean, they have security! I want the same."

"Well, Charlie," the boss replied, "that's asking for quite a lot. I'm not sure we can do that for you. But my wife's my partner. I'll talk it over with her and we'll see what we can provide."

A couple of days later, Charlie was informed that he now had all the insurance he needed plus a healthy pension plan. Wow! Was he motivated! He felt secure in his job and was again the best ditch digger around...for three weeks.

Then, one day, the boss came walking by and there was Charlie leaning on his shovel. To be honest, the boss was perplexed. How could Charlie be dissatisfied? He had good food, warm clothes, a warm place to sleep, health insurance, dental insurance and a terrific pension plan. What more did he need? When questioned, Charlie replied, "Well, boss, I had a chance to get into town on one of the **two** nights off you've given us and I was talking to the guys from ABC Ditch Digging Company. You know, boss, they have a bowling team. Every Christmas they have a party. And besides that, I'm tired of working next to Harry. He has bad breath! I want to work over there, next to Arlene! You see, boss, I have some social needs! I want to feel like I belong somewhere."

The boss replied, "Okay, Charlie, I don't think it would be too difficult to throw together a Christmas party. And we could have an outdoor picnic in the summer and play a little ball. Let me talk to my wife and we'll let you know what we can do."

Did that motivate Charlie? You bet! For about...six weeks. Then, you guessed it, the boss came walking past and there was Charlie, leaning on his shovel.

"How could this be?" the boss wondered, and he confronted Charlie. "What is the problem? We've provided you with good food, warm clothing and a nice, pleasant place to sleep. You have health insurance, life insurance, dental insurance and even a profit sharing plan. You're the captain of the bowling team, chairman of the Christmas party, manager of the softball team and you've married Arlene! For what more could you ask?"

Charlie, leaning on his shovel, scratched his head and said, "You're right, boss, you've been very good to me, but I'll bet I'm the best darn ditch digger you've ever had. As a matter of fact, I believe I'm the best ditch digger in this country. But, does anyone ever say so? Does anyone ever give me a pat on the back? No! I'd like some recognition, you know. Why the other night, I was talking to the fellow down at ABC Ditch Digging Company and they get recognition banquets. They get plaques and sometimes even a gold watch in appreciation of their good work. I never get any gold watches!"

The boss thought it over and after discussing it with his wife, he decided that this was a pretty inexpensive request. So, to keep Charlie happy, he initiated a recognition plan, complete with pats on the back, plaques and gold watches. Surely, Charlie would be satisfied now. Surely, he would be motivated to do the best job he could!

And sure, he was...for about eight weeks, when the boss again found Charlie leaning on his shovel looking bored and dissatisfied. The boss was stunned.

He questioned Charlie, desperate for an explanation. "Charlie, what's wrong now? You have everything a man could possibly want: good food, warm clothing, shelter, insurance plans, pension plans, a bowling team, you're the captain of the softball team, chairman of the Christmas party committee, and you have a beautiful wife, Arlene. You've had your name in the paper every week as 'Ditch Digger of the Week.' You haven't room on your wall for any more plaques. Your arm is covered with gold watches. What do you want now, Charlie? My job?"

"Well, boss," Charlie replied, "that's basically right! You see, I don't feel challenged anymore. I'm the best ditch digger there is and I'm ready for a job where I can find self-fulfillment. I want to be **self-actualized**. I don't know what that means, but I want it!'"

And so we have it: A frustrated worker and an even more frustrated boss. Both are looking for an outside stimulus to create the inner motivation needed for a hard working, conscientious employee. As the story of Charlie illustrates, however, human beings have an unquenchable thirst for more and better things, so that things and rewards and fulfillment of needs are not permanent motivators, but rather temporary movers.

WHAT IS MOTIVATION?

When all is said and done, motivation is an inside job. If a person is truly motivated to accomplish a goal, to be the best in his or her profession or to be a productive and responsible member of society, it is because of a desire that comes from within. The desire remains, even when rewards or recognition are removed. In essence then, a positive, motivated person has a particular thought process that manifests itself in the way he feels, which manifests itself in the way he acts.

Thinking. Feeling. Acting. These three words are primary in defining another word basic to the rest of this **book...ATTITUDE. MOTIVATION IS AN ATTITUDE,** and in the following chapters I will explore the attitudes needed to be a truly motivated and consequently, successful person.

Chapter 2

ATTITUDES ARE CONTAGIOUS... ARE YOURS WORTH CATCHING?

ATTITUDES VS. FACTS

I FIRMLY BELIEVE THAT MOTIVATION IS AN ATTITUDE. Again, I define attitude as the way we think, feel and act. In other words, the way we think determines the way we feel which determines the way we act. This is a simple statement at first glance, but it actually is a profoundly important concept. What this statement is actually suggesting is that your thoughts determine your degree of physical health, the success of family relationships and the extent of success in your career.

Philosophers throughout the centuries have believed in the power of positive thinking. William James said, "Man can change his life simply by changing his attitude." Oliver Wendell Holmes stated it this way, "As you think, you travel." And finally, Ralph Waldo Emerson said, "You are today where your thoughts have brought you. You will be tomorrow where your thoughts take you."

These three men all are expressing the same thing in slightly different ways. But what they are actually saying is summarized in Norman Vincent Peale's statement, "Attitudes are more important than facts." Peale may have been stating his opinion, but there is research that supports that opinion.

In the 1950s a Harvard University study surveyed the four sectors of employment — business, industry, education and government — to determine factors which contribute to an individual's success. They were astounded by the results. It was found that fifteen percent of your success is determined by your attitude!

This statistic started a movement in this country. All areas of employment began to evaluate their training techniques. Were they giving fifteen percent of their training time to developing attitudes? Many business schools, industries and government agencies attempted to increase their percentage of attitudinal training.

Then, in the 1970s, the Andrew Carnegie Foundation funded the largest research study ever done to determine what makes a successful individual. They surveyed more than three hundred thousand people in the four employment sectors. The findings speak for themselves. It was found that seven percent of your success is determined by the knowledge you have, twelve percent by the skills you possess and eighty-one percent of your success is determined by your attitude.

THE INFORMATION EXPLOSION

When you stop to think about it, it really makes sense. When I wrote the first edition of this book the pool of information was doubling every five years. I remember having a conversation with my mother whom was born in 1900. She would reminisce about her childhood days, when travel was by covered wagon. She remembered traveling from Oklahoma to Missouri walking behind the wagon, and being totally frightened by this monster blowing smoke out it's back end. It was her first encounter with an automobile. And yet, she lived long enough to see a man walk on the moon. What change she experienced!

Though she saw a lot of change, **you** have seen more change in the last five years than she saw in a lifetime. And it's not slowing down. A friend of mine who is a futurist stopped me after one of my presentations, where he heard me referring to the rapid rate of information doubling, and said my information was outdated. Information was now doubling every three years. This startled me into looking in the matter in more depth. I found that at the rate we are going, by the year 2002, information will double every thirty-five weeks.

According to the *Wall Street Journal*, at the rate information is doubling, by the year 2008, you wouldn't dare take a three-week vacation. By the time you came back, you wouldn't know enough to do your job! And, by 2015, it will be possible to go to bed smart....and wake up stupid!

So, it will not be possible in twelve to twenty years of formal education to learn all that we will have to know about our profession to prepare us for an entire lifetime. But, if we have a positive attitude about learning, we will continue to update ourselves throughout our careers, getting the knowledge and skills we need to keep up with ever-changing demands.

So you see, attitudes **are** more important than facts.

I'd like to take that one step further. I submit to you that attitudes often create facts. In other words, everything that is created or events that occur, happen first in the mind, as part of a person's thought process, and then it becomes reality.

Let's look at some facts that are well known today. It is a fact that people are burning out on their jobs, and employers are seeking training for these employees to remedy the situation.

It is a fact that many men age thirty-five to forty-five are experiencing a mid-life crisis. It is a fact that there is more absenteeism on Monday that any other day of the week; productivity in industry is lower on Monday than any other day of the week. Is it any surprise that in surveys it has been found that Monday is also the least favorite day of the week?

Are these "facts" beyond our control? Did the sages of old, when determining the calendar, call this day of the week Monday because there would be more heart attacks and absenteeism? Is there some automatic switch that turns on at age thirty-five, that men become dissatisfied and unhappy with their lifestyles? I don't think so.

I believe that people have been listening to a lot of "hogwash" from psychologists, counselors and friends, and they have convinced themselves that this is the way life is.

Let's take a look at this "Monday syndrome." As stated earlier, Monday has been determined to be the least favorite day of the week, the "unluckiest" day of the week. Why? I don't have a lot of hard data to back up my theory, but I do have an idea of how this "fact" came into existence.

This is my scenario. In the same survey I referred to earlier, it was found that Saturday is the favorite day of all seven days, so people want to stay up late on Friday to see this wonderful, terrific day come in. Then they really live it up all day and stay up real late Saturday night to see their favorite day go out. Then, Sunday is recuperation day. Even though people are tuckered out, they can make it through an hour of church (some with the aid of a nap) and then it's time for the Sunday feast.

This ritual reminds me of the last meal that penitentiaries offer convicts before they are executed. You know, this is your last meal. You may have anything you wish and as much as you want. Your one last wish before you die. That's much how we treat Sunday. We eat more than usual, which is known to be bad for our bodies, producing lethargy and poor digestion. We eat a little earlier than usual, which gives us more time in the evening to lie around and "get miserable." I mean, tomorrow is the "execution" day.

I can see it in my mind. Mr. and Mrs. Average American sitting in their living room watching TV. Mrs. says to Mr., "Oh, honey, just think, in only sixteen more hours I have to go back to that awful job and that awful boss for that awful wage. It's making me sick to think about it!"

And Mr. replies, "What are you complaining about? I have to go back in fifteen hours to an awful job that's giving me so much stress I can hardly cope anymore."

They continue to "awfulize" all over each other until finally, Monday morning arrives and they call in sick. Their state of mind created the fact. Or if Mr. goes to work, he has a heart attack in the first stressful situation he encounters. Coincidence? I think not. They have thought, felt and acted their way into the situation.

These people have created a life of misery for themselves. They look forward to the weekend and dread the workweek. In truth, they are two-sevenths people, living only two days out of the week with any pleasure or positive experiences. Is there an alternative? Most definitely! Start working on those attitudes!

IT'S THE LITTLE THINGS THAT MAKE THE BIG DIFFERENCE

There are really only two types of attitudes or thoughts — positive and negative. You can't have a neutral thought. And if you're saying to yourself right now, "Oh, yes I can"...that's a positive thought!

People tell me time and time again that it's hard to be positive in this "lousy" world. And it's not hard to understand why people feel that way. There are plenty of bad things happening in this world, and there are nasty people doing awful things. However, there are plenty of good things happening in this world, and there are good people doing wonderful things.

We know for sure that attitudes are contagious and if we aren't careful of what we look for, whom we associate with and what we feed our minds, it is very easy to focus on the negative aspects of life, to see life as a bad deal.

Let's look at the newspaper for instance. If you read only the front page of the paper, it is certain you will get at least sixty percent negative news. If there are seven stories on the front page, on average, at least four will be negative.

And then, if you watch TV and a typical show such as "As the Stomach Turns," you again see life at its worst. Someone is either in trouble, getting out of trouble or headed for trouble! And the evening news is no different. Even the weatherman contributes to the negative view of life. He reports the weather in the negative. He'll say, "There's a twenty percent chance of rain." Why can't he say it positively? "There's an eighty percent chance it will be a beautiful, sunny day." You see, it's the little difference that makes the big difference.

For example, I was talking with a man from a midwestern city after I had given a presentation there. He had decided he was getting out of that city because the crime rate was up seven percent. This man was an educated professor at the university.

I looked at him and said, "Do you realize what that means? That means that ninety-three percent of the population of this city will not commit a felony or misdemeanor in the next year. Isn't that encouraging?"

He said, "You know, I never really thought of it that way before. It does sound better!"

You see, this negative reporting of the news is warping our sense of reality.

Another statistic that bugs me is the unemployment rate. Even now, when the unemployment rate is considerably lower than it has been at any time in recent history, we still talk about the unemployment rate. Why don't we report the very positive news that ninety-six to ninety-eight percent (depending on what region of the world you are from) of the people who want to work are working? This is a remarkable achievement for our country and it's time we start focusing on **that**.

There is even a positive way of looking at the negative news. By its very definition, news is "something out of the ordinary." If I called the newspaper with the exciting news that while I was out of town, my neighbor came over and mowed my lawn and then left a welcome home sign for me, they'd probably say, "Oh, that's nice. Now what's the news?" You see, people do nice things for other people every day, so this is not extraordinary information, However, if that same neighbor breaks into my house and steals the money out of my cash box, that would be news — because it's out of the ordinary. Actually, we better start worrying when headlines are regularly positive because that would mean that good news is out of the ordinary!

There is room for positive news in the newspaper, but it's normally found on pages three, four and so on. So don't just read the headlines. Dig a little deeper for what's really happening in this world.

Even in our day-to-day lives, it baffles me as to why people must plant negative thoughts in other people's minds, but it happens all the time. If you're susceptible, there will be someone out there who will try to make you miserable. Mothers even get into the act. Every year in September, all over this country, mothers bundle their little children up for school and their parting words are, "Now, don't get run over waiting for the bus!" Is it any wonder that one of the greatest fears youngsters have when they start school is the school bus? They've been led to believe the bus is out to get them! How much better it would be to plant a positive thought such as, "I know you're going to have a wonderful day." It's the little difference...

LOOK FOR THE POSITIVE

If there is any person who understands the importance of planting a positive thought, it is former baseball player Warren Spahn. He still tells the story of the day he was pitching for the Milwaukee Braves in the 1958 World Series. Elston Howard, a dangerous hitter, was next up at bat. Out to the mound walked the Milwaukee manager, who told Spahn, "Whatever you do, don't throw Howard an outside curve. He'll hit it out of the park!" What did Spahn throw? An outside curve and, sure enough, Howard went with the pitch, hit the ball out of the park to bring in the runs that won the series for the Yankees. All Spahn could say to his coach after the game was, "Why did you plant that negative thought in my mind? Why didn't you tell me what

to do instead of what not to do?" It would have made the difference in the outcome of the World Series.

Since those days, psychological studies show that, in fact, our
brain processes messages as either negative or positive. For
instance, if you say to your child, "Don't spill your milk?" the
brain processes, "Spill your milk," and so, that's exactly what happens. However, if you say, "Be very careful with your milk," the
brain hears that positive message in total and the chances are better that the milk will stay in the glass where it belongs.

I guess the classic example of people's tendency to emphasize
the negative, is the true story of the fellow who saw a need for a
new invention. Early in this century, traffic was a real problem in
large eastern cities, with horse-drawn carriages and horseless carriages clogging the streets. It was utter chaos. This man decided
some signals were needed at street intersections to make traffic go
more smoothly. So he built a signal with a green flag, which
allowed traffic to proceed at normal speed, a yellow flag that
meant "caution — slow down" and a red flag that meant "stop
— it's the other fellow's turn now."

As with all inventions he needed to send for a patent. When
he applied for his patent he assigned the name "Go Signal" to
his invention. Go! At the present time, we have very few towns
or cities that don't have these signals, although now we use
lights, but I'll wager you won't find one person in ten who calls
that signal a "go light." We all look at that red light — the neg-
ative-and assume we'll have to stop at every light, so we call it a
"stop light." Yet, less than a century ago, it was patented as a Go
Signal.

If you want to start thinking more positively, the next time you
offer directions to someone, tell them to "go to the third go light

and turn left." I bet you'll at least get a grin out of the other person. And when they ask what you mean, simply reply, "Well, I'm convinced that when you get there, the light will be on green!"

So you see, reality is in the eye of the beholder: You see in life what you look for. Two people can look out of the same window. One sees mud, dirt, dead flowers and dying trees. The other sees blue skies, beautiful sunshine, singing birds and new life sprouting from the ground.

Don't go through life looking in the wrong direction. I once heard a story about a young man named Charlie. He had just turned eighteen and to celebrate, bought himself a new motorcycle. He was so excited about his new bike that he rushed over to the home of his best friend, George. Unfortunately, while on the way there, it began to rain. When Charlie arrived at George's, they decided to go for a ride despite the rain. George got out his raincoat and **decided to put it on backwards** to better protect himself from the pelting rain, using his hood as a shield. (This was in the days before helmets were required.)

They took off on the bike and were having a great time. At one point, Charlie turned to ask George how he liked the ride, but George was gone-he had fallen off the bike. Immediately, Charlie turned around and went back to look for George. It wasn't long before he came upon a crowd of people in the road, and broke through to find George on the pavement in the center of the crowd.

Charlie cried out, "How's George? Is he all right?"

A fellow kneeling over him looked up and replied, "He seemed to be okay when we first got here, but he hasn't said a word since we got his head turned around!"

So, life can be great and positive or dull and negative, depending on which direction we have our heads turned!

Get into the habit of looking for the positive. It may have to be a conscious effort at first. Begin looking for the things you can do in this life rather than those which you can't do. Build on the positive forces in your life. Associate yourself with individuals who are positive. Refuse to allow others to "awfulize" all over you. Instead, start an epidemic of positive attitudes. They are just as contagious as the negative.

ACT — FEEL — THINK!

Remember, you can change your life simply by changing your attitude. How do you change your attitude? You can reverse the process of thinking, feeling and acting. Begin acting more positively today. Use more positive statements like "I love what I do," or "It's a great day." Look for the good in others. Soon you will feel better about yourself, better about what you can accomplish in your lifetime. And when, on a regular basis, you feel better about living, you will then begin to think more positively habitually. It will become an unconscious effort.

In order to maintain that habit, you must daily expose yourself to positive thoughts and experiences. Read books of a positive nature, listen to positive cassette tapes. Do something every day so that the ratio of positive to negative daily experiences will be overwhelmingly positive. Oh yes, you will still encounter negative people and you will still have challenges, but with a positive attitude you can handle those people and challenges more successfully.

I am cautioning you right now, that you will be a different person. People may wonder about you. When you walk into your employee lounge or your planning meeting on Monday morning and say with enthusiasm, "YES, it's Monday! Isn't it great to work here? I've got the greatest job in the world," there may be those who say, "Where have you been? What's wrong with you?" Be strong! Remember that attitudes are contagious and yours will be **worth catching!**

Chapter 3

You Are Worth Millions

Defining Self-Esteem

*S*ELF-ESTEEM IS PROBABLY THE MOST IMPORTANT CHAR-
acteristic of a motivated person. By self-esteem, I
mean the way you feel about yourself — the value you
give to yourself and the confidence you have in yourself. There
are two important parts to self-esteem; self-image and competence. One component impacts the other. I know many people
who are very competent. They are well-educated, skilled people
who have a great deal of talent to share, but don't see it. They put
themselves down and hold back from getting involved because
they think they don't have anything to offer. Their self-image has
not developed to the same level as their competence.

I also know people who have a pretty healthy self-image, even
to the point of telling you how wonderful they are, but truly are
lacking in the competence they need to fully contribute in their
field of endeavor. I am sorry to say that, in the past, many schools
turned out some students whose self-images had been nurtured,

but the school had failed to demand excellence from them and their competency was lacking. (We see things turning around today, thankfully.)

The key is to develop a balance in each area so that, not only are you good, but you know you're good. When you have that, you have confidence and a feeling of self-worth. Now, I am **not** talking about conceit. That's the disease that makes everyone sick except for the person who has it. No, I'm talking about a quiet confidence that comes from knowing you have something to offer this world.

There has been a great deal of controversy about self-esteem and it's meaning. I would like, for the purposes of this chapter to refer to self-esteem as what you feel, see, know and expect of yourself.

THE CAUSE OF LOW SELF-ESTEEM

It seems to me that the older you are the lower your self-esteem. It struck me that in our lifetimes, we hear more about what we are not and can't do than what we are and what we can do. Compliments are scarce, whether it be at home, socially or on the job. And when we finally do get a compliment, we don't know how to take it and we feel obligated to put ourselves down. This might be a typical example:

> "Gee, Maude, that sure is a pretty dress. You look good in it!"
> "What? This rag? I was about to give it to the Salvation Army!"

Why is it so difficult for us to take a compliment? Simple. Because we don't get many of them. In fact, a person who does give a compliment will probably be suspect. The person on the receiving end may very well think, "Oh, oh, what does he want now?"

Our self-esteem is so low we honestly believe we don't deserve the compliment and that it can't possibly be sincere. Why can't we just say thank you and accept it? It might be because most people's lives go something like mine (with a little embellishment).

When I was a boy, I was very much used to hearing these phrases: "No, Dennis." "You can't do that Dennis." "No, Dennis, you're too small, Dennis." Now I heard this a lot, because not only did I have a mom to tell me what I couldn't do, but I also had five older brothers and sisters who felt it was their obligation to make me aware of my limitations. As a matter of fact, many child psychologists say that the average preschool-age child, by the time they're five years old, will hear 20,000 "nos" and only 5,000 "yeses." You don't have to be a Las Vegas gambler to know those aren't good odds — four-to-one negative messages!

I figured school would have to better — my brothers and sisters all looked pretty happy. They even told me I'd like school! (It wouldn't be the first time they lied to me!) School **was** better . . . for **one** year. In kindergarten, I could do no wrong. Anything I did was terrific. Even though my pictures couldn't be deciphered, they were great! I spent hours building block houses and other wonderful creations.

Then I went into first grade and, boy, did things change! Not only did I find out all the things I couldn't do, but my teacher had a red pencil to prove it. I rarely heard about the items on the paper that were right. But there was usually some big deal made about those that were wrong.

In third grade, I took my first test. I got fourteen out of twenty questions right. Pretty good, huh? Not according to my teacher! She made sure there were **check marks** by the ones I got wrong.

Then in fifth grade, I got all but one right on a test and, you guessed it, no mention was made of that fact! As if to say, "You're not perfect — yet," there was that red check mark jumping out at me and a **minus one** at the top of my paper to make sure I didn't misunderstand.

By the time I got into high school I HAD HAD IT! I counted the days until I could get out. Only seven hundred nineteen days. . .only five hundred forty-nine days. . .Finally, graduation day and I could get out into the world of work where I was convinced things would have to be better. My brothers and sisters told me so. (They did it again!) I mean, they had lots of spending money, cars to drive, and time they could call their own. **I was motivated** to get out there and apply for my first job.

I did apply and I was hired. That's when the realities of the "real world" struck again. After thirty days on the job, it was time for my evaluation.

I walked into my boss's office and right away I knew this was not going to be a pleasant experience. I looked around the office and saw a beautiful, plush, high-backed leather chair behind a long, shiny wooden desk. In front of this desk was this little, dented, scratched-up metal folding chair — it was obvious where I was supposed to sit. Then my boss walked in with a somber look on her face, carrying a folder thick with "the goods" on me. She proceeded to inform me of all the terrible things I had done in the course of the last thirty days. I mean, she had it **ALL!** I had taken five extra minutes for lunch on July 10. I was late for work on July 20. I made a mistake on a report on August 1, and on and on. Finally, I couldn't take it anymore. I begged her to stop and I said, "You've convinced me. I'm a terrible worker. I haven't done anything right. How can you keep me on here?"

At that point, she looked at me in surprise and said in these exact works, "Oh, yes, you've done many things right, but I'm not supposed to tell you about that." **I'm not supposed to tell you about that!**

That's when it finally hit me. That is how my mother felt, my brothers and sisters felt, my teachers felt and finally my boss felt. They thought they were helping me by showing me my weaknesses. They were trying to show me how to improve myself. But in reality, they weren't building me up, they were tearing me down, destroying my self-esteem.

Of course, some of us add to our plight by getting married. Somehow, there's often a magic transformation on the day after the wedding ceremony. That person who made you feel so good and believed you could do no wrong, now begins to see your weaknesses and begins to "help" you as well.

"Why is it you always slurp your soup?"

"Slurp my soup? You never minded it before."

"Well, I do now. It sounds terrible and if you don't believe me, ask my mother."

Wow! There are **two** more people to convince you you're less than perfect. Is it any wonder we have a country of people who don't see much value in themselves?

THE SOLUTION

I noted earlier that the reason we find it difficult to accept a compliment is that we aren't used to getting them. . .as illustrated in my "life story." But there is more to it than that. It is also true that the reason we don't **get** many compliments is that we don't give many compliments. Each of us has fallen into the trap of withholding our approval and positive comments from others.

There is an age-old principle that has been stated in various ways. The one I choose to use here is Bob Conklin's version, "To the extent you give others what they want, will you get what you want." What this means to me is simply this: If you feel you would like to start receiving more positive reinforcements and compliments, you must start **giving** them first.

This is a simple concept at first glance, but most people don't want to follow it. They want to reverse the process. Those people who want the principle to operate in the reverse say things like, "If my boss would pay me more, I'd work harder." The boss on the other hand is saying, "If you would work harder, I'd pay you more." The wife says, "I'd appreciate my husband more if he'd only give me flowers more often." The husband is saying, "I'd give my wife flowers more often if she'd appreciate me more." The child is saying, "I'd listen to my parents more if they would listen to me once in awhile." The parent is saying, "If my child would listen to me more often, I might take time to listen to my child."

The hard facts of life show that's "just not the way things work." The principle says that "to the extent you give others what they want **first** will you get what you want." Walk through an exercise with me now to illustrate my point further.

Imagine yourself five minutes after getting up in the morning. You're getting ready to go to work and the phone rings. (Hopefully, you're not in the shower.) You answer the phone, and it's your best friend. He or she begins, "Hi, _____. This is _____. I was just sitting here having my morning cup of coffee and I started to think about you and what a terrific friend you've been, and I realized I've never taken the time to tell you how I feel. So I am doing just that today. Thank you for being my friend. See you Tuesday at bowling."

I can't ask you directly how you'd feel, but I have done this exercise with many people in my workshops and their overwhelming consensus is that they would feel pretty terrific. As a matter of fact, we've done this as an experiment, asking the person's spouse to watch the reaction. They verify the fact that after receiving the phone call, their husband or wife had a lighter spring to their step. They got dressed faster, breakfast was ready earlier than usual. Why? Had anything changed in his or her environment? Not really. But an **attitude** had changed. You have been told by your best friend (one of the smartest people you know) that you are terrific, so you must be terrific and so you act terrific.

Now that's a beautiful story and it probably makes you feel great. But I've got some bad news for you — it's unlikely anyone is going to make that phone call to you. However, **you** can make that phone call. And if you make enough phone calls, **eventually** you may get one.

But that's not really the point. When you make the **first** phone call, you will be getting more than you will be giving. As terrific as your friend will feel when you make that call, you will feel even better, because the getting is in the giving. You will feel like a million bucks, because **you know** you were thoughtful enough to take time out of your busy day to do something to build up someone else and make their day just a bit happier and for that you are **one terrific person.**

43

YOU ARE WORTH MILLIONS!

Speaking of being worth millions, you really are, you know. I'm not speaking about chemicals. In that respect scientists say you're probably only worth about twelve dollars and forty-five cents, maybe more now with inflation. What I'm referring to is your self-worth.

Think about it this way. There was a lady in California who lost her right leg in an automobile accident. She sued the insurance company of the other driver for a million dollars. She won. Would you trade places with that lady? I've asked thousands of people that question and I haven't yet found one person who would. I also read of a man in Minnesota who lost his left leg, up to the knee, in an industrial accident. He sued his company's insurance firm for three million dollars. He won. Would you trade places with him? I think not.

So, you're already worth four million dollars and we haven't even got to the most important part of your body yet. I'm referring to the gray mass between your ears called a brain. The capacity in that one fist-sized area of your body is tremendous. The only catch is, it doesn't work alone — it needs nurturing and it needs to be fed regularly to keep it alert and to fill each cell with new knowledge and fresh positive thoughts that keep the rest of your body moving and motivated.

How valuable is your brain? There are millions of people in this world who would pay millions to have a brain that functions to its fullest capacity. Ask any person with a learning disability or brain dysfunction. Ask the parent of a mentally disabled child.

And yet, often we who have healthy, vibrant brains fail to challenge ourselves to any capacity at all. This is where the competence component of self-esteem comes in. It is up to you to keep updated in your field of work. The attitude that learning is life-long is the attitude that will breed success and competence. Make a commitment to spend as much on learning each year as you spend on your body to look good and smell good. You'll find it will make a difference in your competence, and therefore, confidence and self-esteem.

Caring for Our "Millions"

Albert Einstein once said, "Most people use only ten percent of their brain's capacity. The only reason I'm a genius is because I use thirteen percent of my brain power!"

I don't have to guess what you would do with a car that worked at only ten percent of its capacity. Perhaps you couldn't afford to junk it, but I know you'd at least have it tuned up — give it an overhaul, if necessary.

How often do we treat ourselves to a tune-up of the brain? Take a night course, listen to a tape, attend a workshop, read a book in our professional field or in the area of self-improvement. If you're reading this paragraph, I must congratulate you. You have made an investment in yourself — not only of a bit of money, but also time in the effort to increase your competence. . .and that's great because "you're worth it!"

This attitude of self-esteem is so essential to your success life. And **only you can give it to you** by giving to others; giving your love, your time, your praise. And by taking as much pride in yourself as you do in your own children, or grandchildren, or nieces and nephews.

Suppose one of these young children ran up to you with tear-stained cheeks and said, "I was just playing with some big kids outside and they told me I was a dummy, that I couldn't do anything right. And, you know, I think they're right. I **am** a dummy."

Now would you say, "That's right, dear, and I'm so glad you finally realized it!" Of course you wouldn't. You'd probably gently put your arms around that sad little child and say something like this: "Oh no, honey. You're not a dummy. You can do lots of things right. As a matter of fact, you can do anything you set your mind to!"

Sincere advice. . .when you're offering it to a child. My question is this: As strongly as you can believe in that small child, do you believe that strongly in yourself? How can that small child really believe in what you are saying if you don't believe the same about yourself?

If you are convinced it's important for children to feel good about themselves and feel comfortable and happy with who they are, then it follows that you must believe that for yourself.

Do you truly have good self-esteem? When you can honestly say, "I'd rather be me than anyone else on this earth," then I'd say you're on the right track!

Love is the greatest need anyone possesses. However, your need to give love is as great, if not greater, than the need to receive it. Give yourself some additional self-worth right now - give something to someone that will satisfy your need to give. I promise you, it will come back to you **more than tenfold**.

Chapter 4

"GO WITH GOALS AND HIT YOUR TARGET!"

GOALS VS. PIPE DREAMS

FREQUENTLY, I AM ASKED TO DO WORKSHOPS IN THE area of goal setting. One of the first things I ask people in this program is, "How many of you have goals?" The big majority of people raise their hands.

Then I ask one of them, "Could I see one of yours?"

The usual response from participants goes something like this: "I don't exactly have them with me."

Then I reply, "Well, when you get home, would you send me one of your goals?"

The answer: "Well, I don't exactly have them written down."

My response to that statement **always** is, "If you don't have them written down and you don't have them with you, then you don't have them at all. They're only dreams. . .'pipe dreams,' which usually end up 'down the tubes.'"

Many people in this world go from day to day carrying these

pipe dreams in their minds, foolishly believing that simply by dreaming about it something will miraculously happen. They become like "Tom and Mary" in the following story.

Tom and Mary were high school sweethearts. Everyone knew that one day Tom and Mary would get married, and, sure enough, when they were seniors, Tom and Mary got engaged. They dreamed and planned for their wedding and decided they wanted to go to Hawaii for their honeymoon. They told all their friends, and everyone envied Tom and Mary.

Finally, six months after graduation day, Tom and Mary were married. By this time you, one of Tom and Mary's friends, have moved on to the big city to go to school, but you come home for the big wedding.

When you walk to the back of the church after the ceremony to congratulate Tom and Mary, you say, "Well, I suppose you're off for Hawaii tomorrow."

And Mary replies, "No, we decided to be practical. Both of us are starting new jobs and we have so many expenses right now we decided to wait until we have our feet on the ground."

And you, along with their parents, say, "Oh, that's a wise decision." And life goes on.

Then, four years later, it's time for a class reunion. You see Tom and Mary and you say, "Hey, how was your trip to Hawaii?"

Tom says, "Well, we haven't gone yet. You know, we have little Tom and Mary. And boy, do they need us! But when they get into school and we have a little more time to ourselves, we're going to make that trip to Hawaii." And life goes on.

Years later when you're home to see your parents, you run into Mary downtown. And you say, "Mary! How are the kids **and** how was that trip to Hawaii?"

Mary looks down at the ground and says, "We never went. You know, the kids are in school now and they need us more than ever. Tom Jr. plays ball and Mary is a cheerleader, plus she's on the newspaper staff. So it's run here, run there. There just isn't time to get away." And life goes on.

At your 25-year class reunion (I know the story is getting long, but remember, this is a life story!) you meet Tom and Mary. Surely by this time they've gone to Hawaii. But as you converse with them they confess, "No, we never did go to Hawaii, and now Tom Jr. is just getting settled into a new job. Mary is married and about to have her first child. And you know how the economy is. Mary is going back to work and Grandma and Grandpa are going to babysit. But when our **grandchildren** get in school..."

Did they ever go to Hawaii? Well, the story ends with Tom and Mary (age 92) rocking back and forth on the front porch. Mary looks at Tom with stars in her eyes and says, "You know Tom, I bet Hawaii would have been beautiful. I wish we could have found time to go."

Tom and Mary ended up, like so many of us do, looking back at their lives wishing they would have done what they intended to do when they were young. What is the difference between the doers and the dreamers in this life?

The dreamers are wishing things would happen, hoping that someday they will be walking down the street, kick over a box and find their life's fortune before them. The doers are making things happen, setting goals, planning exactly when and how they are going to accomplish the things they set out to do.

You see, if Tom and Mary had really intended to go to Hawaii and had been doers, they would have set the date for their trip and determined how much money they would need. They would have opened a savings account and begun depositing money on a regular basis to be able to purchase their airline tickets by the date they set. To be really committed, they would even have made room reservations at the hotel they intended to stay in once they arrived in Hawaii — the difference between goals and pipe dreams.

RESEARCH ON THE VALUE OF GOAL SETTING

Why is it that the majority of people do not operate in this manner, setting goals on a regular basis? (Only three percent do.) A study was done at Harvard University to determine what happens to those who do set goals. A survey was done of one hundred students, and it was found that only five of the one hundred set goals on a regular basis, in a systematic manner. (Remember this is Harvard — you would expect a higher percentage.)

Ten years later, a follow-up study was done on these same one hundred people. It was found that the five percent who set goals systematically had ninety-three percent of the total net worth of the group. The other ninety-five had seven percent of the net worth.

We know that the amount of money you have is not the only measure of success, but it is one of the indicators easiest to gauge. However, in the survey, they also found that the five percent who set goals were more satisfied with their family life, were in better physical shape, had received more promotions in their careers and were spiritually more at peace. In the case of the Harvard study, we can conclude that setting goals does make a difference.

And in studying some of the most successful individuals in this country, it becomes apparent that what most distinctly sets them apart from others is that they are or were goal setters. The day Colonel Harlan Sanders of Kentucky Fried Chicken fame died, at the age of 90+, cards with his goals for the month and year were found in his pocket. Goals give meaning to our lives. As Earle Nightingale says, "We must be stretching and growing. Our life only has meaning as we strive to reach new goals." Look at the role goal setting played in the life of Wilma Rudolph, the great Olympic runner. From the time she was told she could never walk, she set a goal to run!

Why Don't We?

So, since we have proof that goal setting can mean the difference in the quality and success of a person's life, why is it that only three percent of the general population sets goals? Why is it that when we run those goal-setting workshops I mentioned at the beginning of this chapter, we have a typically low turnout and even those who do come have difficulty following through with the whole process?

After much research and interviewing many individuals, we have come up with several reasons why people hesitate to set goals.

1. **Many people don't believe they are worthy of success.** Their self-esteem is so low they actually have convinced themselves they only deserve to live from day to day in mediocrity, taking what life throws their way. They actually believe that someone else controls the course of their lives. But even if you're a spiritual person and believe in a Supreme Being, you know that the Father, just as your father here on earth, can only guide you. There comes a point where you have choices to make and you alone

decide which direction to take. And keep in mind that even in the Bible we are reminded to "Love thy neighbor **as thyself**." One of the ways you can really "love yourself" is to get into the goal-setting habit, so that you can live the rest of your life more abundantly. **Believe** you deserve it. Say to yourself, as Ethel Waters, the great gospel singer used to say, "God made me and he don't make junk!"

2. **Many people do not set goals because of a fear of failure.** We hear statements like, "Well, if I set these goals, what if I don't make it? I'll be a failure." And as the chapter on self-esteem points out, we have encouraged the attitude that failure is always to be avoided, at all costs. What a disservice we have done to mankind. Think about it! How many things that you do well now did you do perfectly the first time you tried? From learning to eat, talking, and walking, to driving a car, typing, riding a bike or accomplishing the tasks of your profession, didn't you learn those skills by making mistakes, learning from those failures and trying again? It's the same with any goal you set. I believe that even if you fail to reach your goal, ninety-five percent of the time you'll be further ahead. If you set a goal to lose twenty pounds in six months and you only lose fifteen, haven't you accomplished more than if you hadn't set the goal at all? Aren't you fifteen pounds lighter? Isn't that better than being where you were?

When I was in college, I had a classmate who set a goal to be a millionaire in ten years. When it was time for our ten-year class reunion, all of us were curious to see how our ambitious classmate had done. And you know, he had the nerve to show up and he was worth only $850,000! Of course, we all pointed our fingers at him and said, "What a failure!" **You** know we didn't because he was worth $847,000 more than any of us. Was he a "failure" because he didn't reach his goal or was he further ahead?

Hank Aaron has the reputation in this country for being a success. He held the record for hitting the most home runs in a baseball career. But are you aware that he also nearly broke the record for the greatest number of strike-outs? (By the way, that record was held by Babe Ruth at one time.) But we still consider Hank Aaron one of the greatest success stories of the century. Consider this. Would he have hit as many home runs if he hadn't struck out as many times as he did? Or did he have to fail to succeed? If you talked to Aaron he would probably tell you, "Oh sure, I could have avoided striking out. I could have gone up to the plate and punched at the ball and almost never struck out. But you know what else I'd almost **never** do? I'd almost never hit home runs! You see, in order to hit a home run in the game of baseball, I have to swing hard and **from the heels**."

It's the same thing in life. If you go through the game of life avoiding situations where you might "strike out," you will surely miss the opportunities to hit the "home runs." Vince Lombardi used to say, "It doesn't matter how many times you get knocked down. What really makes the difference is how many times you get back up!" Because when you get back up you could make the tackle that wins the game. Cavett Robert puts it another way: "You won't drown simply because you fall in the water. You only drown if you REMAIN there."

So throw away your "fear of failure" syndrome. Stop letting it prevent you from setting goals for what you really want out of life and remember, "Failure comes before success, even in the dictionary." Use your failures as your stepping stones to success. Let them be your teachers. Learn the lesson that the young man learned when he went to the wisest man in his village and asked him, "Sir, how did you get to be so wise?"

The wise man replied, "With good judgement, my son."

"But," said the young boy, "how did you get good judgement?"

"With experience, my son," replied the wise man.

Persisting, the young boy asked, "And how did you get experience, oh wise one?"

The wise man paused for a moment and then answered most profoundly, "With poor judgement, my son, poor judgement." We learn from our mistakes and failures, and they can teach us the lessons that pave the way to success if we have the right attitude.

3. **Another reason people don't set goals is they don't see the value**. But you're sold, right? You're going to become a habitual goal setter. You believe you deserve success and you're not afraid of failing.

4. This is the point where many people stop, **simply because they don't know how to go about it**, the last **excuse** for not setting goals. I hope the next few paragraphs will remedy that situation so that you may begin to more fully experience life.

The How-To's of Goal Setting

Think of your life as being a long journey. As with any trip, you must know where you're starting from before you can map out where you are going to go. In other words, take an inventory of where you are in the seven areas of your life — mentally, physically, family relationships, spiritually, professionally, socially and financially. How do you do this? Very simply. On seven sheets of paper draw T-graphs and label them in the following manner:

	Strengths	Weaknesses
Physical	1. Balanced diet	5 lbs. overweight
	2. Exercise twice per week	Don't walk enough
	3. Get checkup once per year	Need more regular sleep hours

As I have done here for my physical inventory, list your strengths and weaknesses in each of the seven areas of your total person inventory. (Don't be afraid to let your strengths outnumber your weaknesses — they probably do and should!)

When you have completed this first step, you will have a basis for determining what goals you want to set in each area. I encourage you to look at how you can improve on your strengths as well as how you can eliminate your weaknesses. It is important that you do just that, so that the things you do well are not only maintained, but improved. I say this because chances are you spend the majority of your time doing the things you do well. So doesn't it stand to reason that you should keep improving in those areas? (Especially when referring to your career skills.) If you have problems accepting this idea, think for a moment what this world would be like if every person was constantly working on her weaknesses and no one was utilizing the strengths she possessed.

We would, at best, have a world full of mediocre accomplishments and levels of excellence would fade into oblivion. We **must** have people working in the areas of their strengths to get quality results.

Former professional baseball pitcher Jim Kaat understood this concept through experience. Kaat was, at one point in his career, on the way out — he just wasn't performing up to expected levels. He was pitching for the Minnesota Twins and, fortunately for Jim, he fell into the hands of a pitching coach who understood the value of working on strengths. As was the usual practice, Jim was working out in the bullpen on the first day of spring training. Johnny Sain, his new pitching coach, walked up and said, "What are you doing there, Jim?"

Jim replied, "I'm working on my changeup."

Sain said, "Why, Jim?"

And Jim explained, "Well, that's my worst pitch and I really need to work on it."

Johnny Sain immediately corrected Jim Kaat. "No, Jim, you've got it all wrong! What is your **best** pitch?"

"My fastball," Jim said, a bit puzzled.

"WELL, doesn't it make sense that your fastball should be better than it is now?"

Jim bought what Johnny Sain had to say and began practicing his fastball a majority of the time. And it must have worked. That year Jim Kaat won the Cy Young Award and just about every other award a pitcher can win.

Now it may be a surprise to you, but later Jim Kaat's best pitch became his changeup. How did that happen? Here's how. Imagine Jim Kaat up on the mound ready with his awesome fastball. He pitches his first fastball — "Strike One!" He pitches his second fastball, "Strike Two!" The batter is totally frustrated. Now, if you know anything about baseball, you know that when a pitcher has a batter down two strikes and no balls, it's time to throw a waste pitch — the weakest pitch that the pitcher throws. For Jim Kaat, as you recall, that was his changeup. But now, when Jim throws that changeup, he's doing it from a **position of strength**. He isn't concentrating on practicing something he was weak in; he is throwing his weakest pitch to throw off the balance of a batter he already has down 0 and 2. And more than that, if this situation occurs with every batter in the game, he's going to throw his changeup at least twenty-seven times in that game. Now you can understand why, in his last few years in baseball, one of Jim's best pitches was his changeup. It's obvious.

And yet in the game of life, how many of us are throwing our **fastball**? How many of us even know what our fastball really is? That's what taking an inventory of our strengths and weaknesses is all about. Looking for our fastballs and then using them. And, if we work on that fastball often enough, we may just make those changeups (weaknesses) more effective as well.

Once you have your self-inventory done, it's time to start thinking about the trip of life again, but now you need to determine your destination. The question you must answer first is, "What is my purpose in life?" That's a tough question to answer, but it's an all-important one. Do you want to be remembered for your generosity, or your service to mankind, or your ability to bring happiness into other's lives? What **do you** want to accomplish in your lifetime? This is what is called your **mission statement.**

When you have written that down, as you should write down all your goals, it is time to determine the route you are going to take to that ultimate destination.

THINK BIG

Before we go any further, I'm going to encourage you to think big when you are doing your planning. Again, don't worry about failing to reach your goal, because most likely, if you've set that goal high enough, even if you don't reach it, you'll be farther ahead. Remember the story of my classmate who had a goal to be a millionaire? What if he had set a goal to make only $500,000? Would he have quit once he got there?

It's kind of like the farmer who ordered a dozen chickens from the general store. The farmer wasn't going to be home when the chickens arrived so the store owner had them delivered in a crate to the front of the house. Later the farmer called the store owner and said, "I guess it wasn't such a good idea to have the crate delivered when I wasn't here. When I got home, the crate had broken and chickens were all over the place! It took me all day to round them up and even then I only found eleven."

The store owner replied, "Well, that ain't bad, cuz I only left six!" If the farmer had known that only six chickens had been left, he would have quit after six, but he had a **bigger goal** in sight, and because of that he **was farther ahead**. As Leo Hauser, a personal friend and speaker says, "Shoot for the moon! Even if you miss, you'll land among the stars." Having grown up on a farm, I say "Most people shoot for the barn door. Then if they miss you know what **they** land in!" So think big as you set your goals. Don't allow yourself to wallow around in the mud and murk of life because you haven't given yourself enough of a challenge.

MAPPING YOUR LIFE'S JOURNEY

Okay, what route are you going to take to arrive at your life's purpose? Look again at each area of your life and set a ten-year goal.

As you set this goal, check to make sure it is in direct correlation to your mission statement. Where do you want to be in ten years physically, in your mental development, career-wise, spiritually, financially, in your social relationships and in your family relationships? Be sure to consider your self-inventory. Remember to concentrate on your strengths to improve them, and choose one weakness to improve upon. For example, you may be in pretty good physical condition, but you want to maintain and even improve your condition. Your goal may be to be a size 10 (women) or to fit into pants with a 32 waist (men). Mentally, you may want to earn one hundred credits at the local university or read the top fifty books in the area of self-development or in your professional area. Notice that these goals are beginning to be more specific. The closer to the present time you get the more specific your goals should be.

Have you written down your ten-year goals? If not, take time to do it, right now!

Now it's time for your five-year goals. You arrive at these by looking at your ten-year goals, and determining what must be done in five years to reach your ten-year goal. You're going to earn one hundred credits in ten years. That breaks down to fifty credits in five years. You're going to have 4,000 hours of meaningful communication with your wife and children in ten years. That means you must have 2,000 hours in five years. Again, do this in each of the seven areas of your total-person development.

We are now ready for one-year goals. Based on your five-year goals, what must you do in one year? If you want to save $5,000 in five years, that means $1,000 in one year. You're going to be a size 10 in ten years. How much weight do you have to lose in one year to get there? How many hours of exercise will you have to do? Be specific. The goals you are writing down must be measurable, so that at the end of one year you can determine whether you have reached your goal or not.

I'm sure you have the system now. Break those one-year goals down to six-month goals. Are you still with me? Or have you stopped planning because we're getting too close to home? If you're still with me, actually writing down your goals, consider yourself special. You are in that three percent of the population that set goals on a regular, on-going basis.

But we're not done yet. Now take your six-month goals and break them down to one-month goals, then one-week goals and finally set your goal for what you must do **today** to begin arriving at each of your goals.

Do It Now!

Don't read on until you've accomplished all these steps. I'm taking a real risk making that statement because I know how threatening it is to set goals for what we must do right now. You see, most people run their lives like a track race. They line up on the starting line ready to run, seeing that far-away destination. Then it's time to start, and it's "one for the money, two for the show, three to get ready, four to get ready. . .five to get ready. . .six to get ready. . ." They're always **getting ready** but they **never go!** Don't be one of them! Set that goal for this day and this moment and go!

As you get started, you may find you set some of your goals too low. You may reach them more quickly than you had planned. That's great! But don't quit there. Set another goal in that area. Setting goals is much like climbing a hill. Once you reach the top of one hill you can see a new horizon, a new hill to climb. Go for it.

Don't ever be satisfied with where you are. I hope that you have a desire to spend your whole life growing, improving and learning. Because if you're not growing, you're dying. There is no standing still in life. Remember that success in life is not a destination but a journey. We are always striving to be more successful than we are. That's how this country got to be the great country it is. It's up to each of us as individuals to keep it that way.

So now you have your goals written down. They are meaningful and specific. They relate and are in direct correlation to your lifetime goal or purpose, and you will be able to evaluate how successfully you have reached them.

The 3 V's of Goal Setting

There are "three V's" you must keep in mind as you set about accomplishing these goals.

The first V is to **Verbalize** your goals. Tell yourself aloud what you are going to do. State it in positive terms. "I am a size 10." "I will save $3.50 a day!" "I do read one hour a day in my career area." But don't stop there. After you tell yourself, tell someone you can trust what you plan to do so they can help you reach your goal. Tell enough people so that they, along with you, believe that you mean business.

At the same time you're verbalizing, you can be doing the second V. **Visualizing.** Actually see yourself doing or accomplishing the goal you set. See yourself with your doctorate diploma in your hand; see yourself as a size 32 waist; visualize your savings account book with $10,000 written in the credit column.

The final "V" is probably the most difficult for people to accomplish. That is to **Vitalize** — actually do what you said you want to do.

Earlier in this chapter, I listed reasons for failing to do this. Don't allow those reasons (excuses) to stop you. Believe you deserve to reach your goals. Don't be afraid of failure. Remember, even when you fail, it brings you closer to success. The only people that never fail are people who never do anything. Finally, you know how to set goals and, hopefully, by the time you read this sentence you have gone through the steps and are ready for the element which determines the success of all your efforts. **Vitalization.** Don't wait for next Monday or next month to start. Don't procrastinate. The last three words I leave you with in this chapter are the three words which state most simply one of the greatest laws of success, "DO IT NOW!"

Chapter 5

YOU'VE GOT A PROBLEM — THAT'S TERRIFIC!

GETTING A PERSPECTIVE

*A*S WE LOOK AT PROBLEMS, I'M REMINDED OF THE story they tell about Charlie and his cat. Charlie was single and the one thing in the world that he was attached to was his cat. His company asked him to go to Europe and open a branch office. He called his younger brother George, who was still living at home with their mother, and asked if he could leave his cat there while he was gone for the four- to five-week period. His younger brother agreed. Charlie had been gone about four weeks when he was informed that things were going so well his company wanted him to open another new location in Europe. He called home and said to his brother, "This is the situation, George. They want me to open another office. It looks like I'll be another five or six weeks. By the way, how's my cat?"

"The cat's dead!"

"The cat's dead?" Charlie replied. "You know how I've grown

to dearly love my cat. Here I am thousands of miles from home and you just blurt out all at once, 'The cat's dead!' You could have been a little sensitive and said the cat's on the roof. Then when I called next week you could say the cat fell off the roof and broke his leg. Then the next time you could have said that we took the cat to the vet and due to the severity of the injury and age of the cat, we had to put the cat to sleep. But no, not you! You just tell me, 'The cat's dead.' Well, I guess the damage is done now. By the way, how's mother?"

"Oh...Mother's on the roof," replied George. (Tact and diplomacy aside, that story puts problems in perspective, doesn't it?)

PROBLEM VS. OPPORTUNITY

When we talk about problems, we have to identify whether or not we really have a problem. A problem for one person may not be a problem for another. I have observed people in similar work situations. One is vibrant and energized by the challenge of their work. The other is stressed out because of the perceived insurmountable problems that they have to deal with on a daily basis. The difference? Attitude!

You've got a problem? That's terrific! Problems give you a chance to live, grow and improve. Every problem is an opportunity to grow and learn. That is the only positive way to look at problems. I don't like problems any more than the next person, but I'm going to get them anyway. So why not take a positive approach to them? Think to yourself, every adversity contains the possibility of an equivalent or greater opportunity and every problem contains the seeds of its own solution. But you will never find that seed if you allow yourself to be overwhelmed by your circumstance.

Consider this. Tomorrow you ought to be better than you are today. That's what growth is all about. Problems, and the solutions to them, provide us with that growth — improvement and change that will make you stronger, smarter and greater than you are today. My philosophy is, "If I can't be better tomorrow than I am today, why stick around?" When you cease to grow, you begin to die. Even if I was physically unable to do what I do today, I could still find ways to learn, grow and contribute to my community or any other group who might benefit from my skill and knowledge.

To me life is worth living only if we grow, improve and stretch. Boredom and apathy set in the moment growth stops. Pessimism is the next step. Think back to the summer vacations you spent during your school years. You will have to admit that by the end of the summer you were bored and ready to return school. I have seen the same situation with retirees, if they retire to nothing. It sounds so wonderful to have absolutely nothing to do, no problems to solve, no pressure. But the truth is, after a few months of the life of leisure, most people start looking for ways to get involved with life again. They actually look for problems they can help solve — even if it's on a strictly volunteer basis. You see, life has nothing to offer us if we have nothing to offer life.

You won't solve all the problems you encounter in life, but in attempting to solve them you grow stronger. Some of the problems we face such as dishonesty, lack of integrity, and immorality can't be solved totally by any of us, but we can grapple with them and try to improve things — make them a little better and, in the process, we come away from that confrontation a better man or a better woman than before.

THE MEASURE OF OUR WORTH

Human beings can be measured by the size of the problems they confront. The bigger and more problems you have, the more alive you are. Problems constitute life! We go through school learning to solve problems in preparation for life. In first grade we have first grade problems, in fifth grade the problems are harder. By the time we reach high school, the problems are pretty tough. Then, we finally graduate and expect and desire no problems. This is not realistic. School was preparing us to solve problems!

Life is not always a bowl of cherries. As Erma Bombeck said, "Some days it's the pits." It's how we deal with the pits that is important. We can't control all the things that happen to us, but we can control our reaction to these things. That's a healthy attitude toward problems. We can choose to let problems overcome us, ruin our day and cause us stress, or every day we can choose to give thanks for the problems in our life. Because of your company's "problems," you've got a job. And the bigger the problems you are able to solve for your company, the better job you have, with more compensation for what you do! Your family has problems that give you purpose in life-a reason to get up in the morning.

PEOPLE PROBLEMS

Most of our problems are caused by other people, aren't they? Other people would love to pull your strings, control your life. There are negative people who would love to make you miserable — if you give them permission. As Eleanor Roosevelt said, "No one can make you angry without your permission. Why would you give it to them?" Think of it. "Anyone who angers you, conquers you," according to Sister Kenny of the Kenny Foundation. The moment you give someone else control of your feelings and actions, you have given up control of your life.

If you ask anyone to list all their problems on a sheet of paper, you would find that most of the problems listed are problems caused by other people. Get rid of the person causing the problem, some people believe, and you get rid of the problem. Probably well over ninety percent of our problems are people problems.

How do you deal with people problems? According to the late Bob Conklin in his program "Adventures in Attitudes," there are three basic ways that most of us try to deal with people problems. The first method we use is to **change the situation**. You don't like the neighbor because he's got a dog that does things in your yard - move! You don't like the way the boss talks to you — quit your job! You're unhappy because your spouse snores — get a divorce! However, the attitude "I'll change the situation and that'll eliminate my problems' has never worked very well. Problems have a way of following you wherever you go. Dr. Russell Conwell in his book, *Acres of Diamonds,* tells of "Changeable Chester." He goes through life changing jobs, locations, wives, etc., in a never-ending search for success. He never changes Chester, however.

So changing the situation is generally a very impulsive and immature solution to a problem. That doesn't mean we should never quit our job, never move to another location or obtain a divorce. It does mean there is usually another alternative. But so often we react emotionally and then try to justify our actions with facts instead of getting the facts and then reacting logically.

That brings us to our second method of solving people problems. **Change the other person.** This may be the secret desire of everyone whether we'll admit it or not. This may be the motivation behind lots of people buying books on how to influence others. Then they are disappointed because the book, if it is a good one, talks about changing yourself. The reader is hoping to pick up a "secret formula" for dealing with others. They are hoping the book will tell you how to walk up to the person you are having the problem with, say the secret words, sprinkle a little whiff 'n' poof dust on them and presto! They'll undergo a major transformation and start agreeing with you on everything.

Do you really believe this can be done? Of course not! It simply won't work. Even if you prove them wrong, you may win the battle and lose the relationship. People don't like to be wrong. Remember the last argument you had? You were right, weren't you? And you can prove it, too, can't you?

I remember an experience from my childhood days. My sister and I were having an argument about a certain topic. I said it was one way...she said another. This kept up until I looked it up in the encyclopedia and I was right! I showed her the "right information" in front of the whole family. She slapped me and said, "The book is wrong!" See what happens when you prove the other person wrong?

Perhaps I would have been successful if I had kept my mouth shut and waited for her to come to me after looking up the answer. Possibly she would have said, "Well, little brother, you were partially right!" Instead we both ended up trying to defend our positions so we would "be right."

So changing the other person is not the best solution. Change can only come from within the person. It must be their decision and even then change is slow and difficult.

This brings us to the third method of dealing with people problems: **Change your attitude toward the person creating the problem for you.** You can't change the other person's attitude, so you're left with this alternative. Look at the situation and determine what YOU can do to remedy the situation. Ask yourself if you are contributing to the problem in any way, and then seek to change what you can about yourself. It may not seem fair, but life isn't fair and it does have the homely virtue that it works!

THE POWER TO FORGIVE

You have a great advantage over a person who does you an injustice: you can forgive them. They don't have that advantage. Why, you might even have a chance to hear the words that all of us want to hear — "I'm sorry, I was wrong. I made a mistake. Will you forgive me?" Certainly, we can say those words even if we don't hear them as often as we think we should. Mahatma Gandhi said, "The weak can never forgive. Forgiveness is an attribute of the strong." And the more you forgive, the stronger you will be.

I'm reminded of the workshop I attended many years ago on anger and hostility. The speaker suggested that when you feel anger and hostility, let the other person know it in no uncertain terms. If you don't like the way you were treated let 'em have it. The waitress upsets you — tell her off! Don't hold it back!

I talked to the presenter at the break and explained to him that I was leery because I was taught some time ago that if you have something that works in your life hang on to it. If you've got something that doesn't work get rid of it. I found out that getting angry at people didn't work for me. They got angry back!

I've got a better idea: Why not be nice to people? Love them even when they're not lovable. It'll take a heap of doing — but it works so much better. It eliminates much of the stress you otherwise feel. Anger is not normal when displayed. Note how those around you change when they get angry. They're not the same person at all, are they?

Usually we fight changing ourselves, don't we? We go to the doctor when we have pain and ask to have the pain relieved. Give me a shot or a pain reliever. The pain is still there, but you don't feel it anymore.

Maybe we need to find out what causes the pain and quit doing that. But that means changing ourselves again, doesn't it? It's so much easier to get the quick fix, especially in today's world of pain relievers for everything. You don't have to feel the pain. But can you learn from pain? Of course! You can learn that something isn't working right in your life, so you can change it. Perhaps it's too much coffee, too much alcohol, or poor diet choices.

We need to stop making those choices, not be relieved of the painful results of poor choices. Often we learn from the pain. There's pain in living, there's pain in dying...but you can learn from the pain and then use that lesson to make your life better.

A PROBLEM-SOLVING SYSTEM

It's easier to be positive about problems if we have a systematic way of solving them. In other words, we need to be good problem solvers. We grow from the problem we try to solve. Here is a seven-step process you can go through when you have a big problem to solve. Obviously you don't go through the process with every decision you make, but it will help you with many of the major challenges in your life.

Step #1: Define the Problem

We often try to solve the result of a problem rather than the problem itself. We have to determine the cause of a problem as well as the result of a problem. Dealing with the cause is more likely to resolve the problem than dealing with the result.

Absenteeism in the workplace is a problem. To solve that problem we have to determine what **caused** this absenteeism (which is a result of the problem). It could be a problem in the person's personal life, illness, relationship problems or problems with children. It could even be the attitude of the supervisor.

Putting on your clothes and finding that they no longer fit is a problem. What caused the problem? Though we would all like to think the clothes shrunk, typically the problem is too many bites of food. The solution isn't to go out and buy bigger clothes when the problem is defined in this way. The solution is to eat less or become more active, right?

Step #2: Analyze the Problem

A.   Assemble all the facts you can. You'll never have all the facts but assemble all you can get.

B.   Determine what factors are influencing the problem.

1.   Internal factors (directly relating to the problem like financial issues, stress, lack of communication, etc.).

2.   External factors (not directly relating to the problem but affecting it, like attitudes of the people involved, perhaps a personal problem that prohibits you from focusing on the problem).

Step #3: Develop Alternative Solutions

This is like brainstorming! Try to get as many alternatives as possible. At this point don't be too concerned about the quality of the solutions; you'll deal with that in the next step. Just be creative. Think outside the norm. Write down all possible solutions no matter how silly they may sound.

Step #4: Evaluate Each Alternative

A. What's the risk of each alternative? Is it worth the risk or is the problem not of enough significance to risk this particular alternative? Sometimes a problem may not be significant enough to really stick your neck out.

B. What is the probable outcome of each alternative solution?

Step #5: Select One Solution

Now choose one of the alternatives, taking into consideration the following:

A. Past Experiences — If you've had a similar problem before, how did you handle it? What have you learned in the past about this problem? Will a similar solution be effective this time?

B. Hunches — this is the "gut" feeling or inspiration that we all get in some situations. Something tells us this is the right way to go. It's not the most objective method, but many great decisions have been made this way.

C. Advice from Others — We can learn from the experiences of others and we do need each other. Other people who have had the same problem may be glad to share what they have learned. Others often have an insight we lack because we're too immersed in the situation.

D. What do you want as the final outcome?

E. Prayer — You should never attempt to solve any major problems without the help of Almighty God. Who do you think you are that you can do it by yourself? Pray hard and work hard on the problem.

Step #6: Apply the Solution

This is critical. Analyzing and contemplating problems do no good, unless we put our solutions to the test. It may be risky, but you will be glad you tried when the problem is solved.

Step #7: Evaluate the Solution

A. If it works, you've solved the problem. There are probably other good solutions, but you've found one that works — hang on to it.

B. If it doesn't work, go back to Step #5 and select another solution. Don't believe that you only have one chance to solve a problem. We get good judgement from experience and we get experience from poor judgement. We learn (sometimes even more) from an unsuccessful attempt at solving problems. It's only when we don't try that we learn nothing at all.

So there you have it. When you learn about problem-solving techniques, develop the know-how to use a system, and cultivate the attitude that every problem is an opportunity to learn and grow, you too, will be able to say "Hey, I've got a problem — that's terrific!"

Chapter 6

BELIEVE AND ACHIEVE

THE KEY TO MOTIVATION

ACHIEVEMENT HAS ALWAYS BEEN GREATEST WHEN ONE is involved in doing something one really believes in. Belief is truly the key to motivation. It has been defined as the "substance of things hoped for; the evidence of things not seen." Faith is another word for belief.

Belief is an attitude that each of us can learn and develop. How do we do this? Begin by identifying your current beliefs and where they come from. Do you believe in something just because everyone else does, or have you identified your passion — your purpose — your mission in life? Have you thought about what you want to remember about your life? When you look back in old age, what do you want to see? What will create a sense of fulfillment and peace for you?

If you can't answer these questions, you can certainly be led down a path that will not bring maximum achievement and fulfillment, but mediocrity. The so-called "average" person is not what I suggest you strive to be, but rather the leader...the believer...the doer...the person who is making a difference in some way, large or small. To strive for excellence is what this book is all about.

Our beliefs shape not only what happens in our lives, but to a great extent the length of our lives as well. Dr. Dennis Waitley says that our expectations create a self-fulfilling prophecy that may even include how long we are going to live. He states that we determine at an early age how long we believe we will live, and then live accordingly to make sure we are right.

COMPONENTS OF BELIEF

The ability to believe is based on several components. Obviously you must have knowledge about something in order to believe in it. It's much easier to believe and understand the Bible, for example, if you "know" the author and have studied the subject. It is easier to believe in the work you do if you understand how you fit into the larger goals of the company. When you understand the "piece of the puzzle" you contribute to the goals and objectives of the organization, it helps you to see that you are important to the organization.

This knowledge must be strengthened by a consistency that is based on past experiences. We believe, for example, that the eggs we buy in the store come from chickens. Why? Because every other time we bought eggs before, they were chicken eggs, so our past experience tells us to expect the same. But would it be different if we cracked open an egg purchased from the store and a turtle fell out? Would we still totally believe or might we check those eggs every time to make sure? Our trust level has been lowered and therefore our ability to believe.

So, belief is knowledge and belief is trust that comes from consistent experience over time.

With knowledge, consistency and trust, the ability to believe is developed. That belief becomes so strong that non-believers and circumstances cannot tear down or destroy this belief. In other words, if it is really something a person believes and values, he or she will act on it consistently over time. You will not waver with the prevailing winds of opinion, but rather hold to that which you believe to be right. Faith is built in this manner.

BELIEF LEADS TO ACHIEVEMENT

David Sarnoff, founder of RCA, said that "whatever the mind of man can conceive and believe, it can achieve." This means your beliefs are not imposed on you by someone else, but you can cultivate your beliefs and life expectations based on information you receive from many different sources. And when your mind can conceive or create the idea and you are able to truly believe in the idea based on input from your own research and the input of others, then it is possible for you to put forth the effort to achieve your dream or your goal.

I like to be a positive source of information for those who have lost their ability to believe. I remember one incident where I tried to increase the belief of one who seemed to have lost her zest for her work and life in general. She was a waitress in a restaurant where I had gone to have breakfast with two of my associates. It was evident she did not believe in her importance to the organization from the behavior she exhibited.

My associates and I arrived just as the restaurant was opening. We were, in fact, their first customers. The sign said, "Please seat yourself," so that's what we did. It's a good thing, too, because we would have been waiting a very long time to be seated otherwise. We saw someone peek over the kitchen window/counter area and then duck their head, as if hoping that we hadn't seen them. Didn't they want our business?

Finally, a less-than-enthusiastic young lady came shuffling out of the kitchen door. If you remember the Tim Conway skits where he played the old man barely able to get from one side of the room to the other, you will have a good idea of the gait and shuffle of this young lady! Eventually, she got to our table. She sullenly asked us what we wanted for breakfast.

At this moment, I decided I was going to make a difference for this young lady. I said to her brightly, "Good morning! Isn't it a great day?

She scowled at me and said, "Oh, don't say that. Now I feel even worse."

I said, "What do you mean?"

She answered, "Oh, I'm having a bad day. (The day had just started!) I'm only working here because I can't find any other job, and I'm just not happy."

This lady seemed in dire straits, but I was determined to help her. I replied, "Tell you what. Why don't you go get us four cups of coffee?"

She raised one eyebrow and said, "Okay, I'll get the coffee, but why four cups?"

I explained, "Well, three cups are for us and one is for you. You don't look overwhelmed with business this morning (they weren't even whelmed), so you'll have time to sit for a minute. When you get back with the coffee, I'll give you five reasons why you should be happy."

She said, "Oh, okay. But I don't know what you can say...I'm pretty unhappy."

Now, if I had known how long it would take to get the coffee, I could have come up with ten reasons! She must have walked into the kitchen, out the back door, taken a taxi to the airport, got on the plane, flew to Columbia, climbed the mountain, picked the beans, flew back, roasted and ground the beans, made the coffee and THEN brought it to us. We waited a l-o-n-g time!

She got to our table a little quicker than she had the first time. I think she was curious to see what I had to say. She said, "Here is your coffee. Now, what is it you think I should be happy about?"

I thought to myself, "Ok, here we go!"

I said, "Alright, number one, you're young. (Age doesn't really determine your happiness, but she was young and should be happy about that!)

"Number two, you're pretty. (Beauty isn't necessarily a factor in happiness, but she was endowed with a good share of beauty and needed to appreciate that fact.)

"Number three, you have a job. (That does have something to do with being happy. When you are able to be productive and can contribute to your own welfare and the success of others, that is a cause for celebration. Many people can't even find a job due to a lack of skill or ability.)

"Number four, you live in the greatest country in the world, where you are free to make choices about how you live your life. (Check out the number of countries where this is not true!)

"And, number five....you have a customer like me at 6:30 in the morning!"

Well, she didn't do cartwheels, but she did walk away with a smile on her face, a little lilt to her step and when she brought us our food, she was actually humming a tune. I'd like to think I helped her believe in herself and her purpose in life just a little bit more.

But if I didn't, at least I contributed to my ability to believe in my mission. There it is again...To the degree that you give others what they need, will you get what you need. It really works.

Many motivational experts trace the cause of low motivation to the fact that people are losing their ability to believe. Some people believe in their voluntary organizations more than their jobs. This probably further proves that money doesn't motivate, but the ability to believe in something does. If we can recapture the ability to believe, we can lead more satisfying and productive lives. If you go to work every day to a job you don't believe in, certainly it will produce stress and a very negative environment.

If David Sarnoff was right about belief, then the word "impossible" couldn't exist in our vocabulary. We would be limited only by the extent of our beliefs.

In the 1950s, sports and medical experts all over the world told us that one thing was surely impossible: running the four-minute mile! Many went to great lengths to explain that the body could not possibly endure such strain. Why, it was said the body would literally burst!

But they didn't count on the power of the mind - the ability to believe. One young man, who obviously hadn't read all the articles, just went out and ran the mile in less than four minutes.

It had never been done before but it has been done over and over again since. Why? Why is it that nobody could do it before Roger Bannister, but running the four-minute mile became a common occurrence after Bannister? All of a sudden people had more physical ability? Was training improved overnight? **Or** were the limitations simply removed from the minds of the participants? Surely the latter is the case. Whatever the **mind** of man can **conceive** and **believe**, it can achieve. People began to know (step #1) that it could be done, they saw it happen (step #2 — consistency and past experiences), and they trusted their own abilities to accomplish the same thing (step #3). When the impossibility is removed from the mind, it is removed from the physical reality.

Years later Roger Bannister was asked to discuss his seemingly amazing achievement, the four-minute mile. His response was that "all barriers are self-imposed and I was the first to really believe it could be done." He created the belief for others by doing it himself. Then they could do it (achieve).

Clarence Blaiser says you must run your own "four-minute mile." He is talking about removing mental barriers that hold you back, limit your beliefs and retard your success. Perhaps there is no goal unreachable if our ability to believe is strong enough. Many of us live in a prison of our own making. We escape from that prison by changing our beliefs. A lot of people say, "I'll believe it when I see it." The truth is closer to, "You would see it if you believed it."

Can someone run the mile in three minutes someday? Roger Bannister says, "of course they can." When? When they believe it. One can't conceive and believe of going from four minutes to three minutes just like that. We can, however, conceive of going from 3:59 to 3:58 to 3:57 to...a progressive realization of the three-minute mile. We have to be able to conceive it in our minds before we believe it and then we can achieve it. Dr. Robert Schuller, a noted pastor, says, "By the yard things are hard, but inch by inch anything's a cinch."

There are some doctors today who tell us that by the year 2020 there may not be any doctors. The healing may come from the mind. We don't know exactly how it will be done because we don't presently have that ability, but as we learn more about the human mind it may happen - when we begin to believe it is possible.

The power of the mind has led to some very amazing results. There is the story of the young high school golfer who shot in the 80s; then he was drafted and sent to Vietnam. There he was captured and spent several years as a POW. Each day as a prisoner he spent time golfing, in his mind. The result was that he got pretty good; he was shooting in the mid-60s in his mind. After being released and sent home he was debriefed and allowed to rejoin his family. The first weekend home he went golfing and shot in the low 70s — nearly 10 strokes better than he had ever shot before! You see, he had been golfing every day in his mind even though he had not been on a real golf course in several years!

The mind doesn't know the difference between a real event and one that is imagined. Whatever you conceive becomes reality if it continues to be conceived in your mind. Muhammed Ali used this type of programming of his mind all through his boxing career. He literally brainwashed his own mind by filling it full of positive expectations that he was indeed the greatest!

BELIEVE MORE IN YOUR WORK

What would happen to us on the job if we began to believe more deeply in what we do? Sometimes there is value in taking a few minutes to mentally go through a process that can stimulate a deeper belief.

Many of us have probably wished we could quit our jobs at one time or another. Be honest — haven't you? Well, go ahead and do it — mentally. I suggest that you quit your job — mentally — on the weekend or one day after work.

Then reapply for your job. Good news! You're hired! You get to go to work tomorrow! Call up someone. Tell them you got the job. Celebrate. You did when you first got your job, didn't you?

Now imagine that tomorrow when you return to work it is your first day on the job. Remember that feeling? What would happen if we could keep that first-day feeling every day? Would our belief be just a little stronger?

Think of the ways you would personally benefit by believing more in your job. "Less stress," "more enthusiasm," "the day goes faster," "more interest," "higher productivity," are some of the responses I have gotten over the years at workshops. Whatever the benefits, the ability to believe is the key.

Research tells us we will work hard for money. We will work harder for a leader we believe in, but we will work hardest for a cause we believe in. Find a way to make your work your cause.

AVOID "DREAM KILLERS"

One thing we have to avoid to keep a deep belief is the dream killer. That is, the negative thinker who is working to kill your ability to believe. This person will chip away at your belief every day in an attempt to kill it. He or she will say things like "I used to be an idealist, too, but you've got to be realistic." In other words, you're only realistic if you're a negative thinker, according to the dream killers. They do not know that reality is "belief activated." William James says, "Our belief creates the facts." If belief was not so powerful, how do you think God planned to make Christianity work?

Your ability to believe will create your reality. Fear can literally kill or incapacitate a person, yet fear is based on what you **believe** will happen, not what has already happened.

Whatever you vividly conceive, ardently desire, sincerely believe, and enthusiastically act upon...will come to pass in your life. "If thou canst believe, all things are possible to him that believeth." (Mark 9:23)

Chapter 7

LIFE IS TERRIFIC — GET WITH IT

A CRITICAL ATTITUDE FOR MOTIVATION

*I*F I WERE TO ASK YOU TO LIST CHARACTERISTICS INHER-
ent in a motivated person, enthusiasm would be at or
near the top of the list. Enthusiasm is an attitude that
is critical to a highly motivated individual.

It is the most visible of all attitudes and it is the easiest attitude
to develop. To be enthusiastic, you only need to act enthusiastically. The action will bring about the being. An attitude is defined
as the way we think, feel, and act. We can change our attitude
more by changing our actions than we can by changing our
thinking. In fact, changing our actions over a long period of time
(at least twenty-one days),will often result in a change in attitude.
Enthusiasm can be developed just as every other attitude or habit
is developed — through practice.

You may not be able to determine how someone thinks and
feels by looking at them, but you make a judgement about their
attitude based on how they act. So, those who are thought to be

motivated people are those that are enthusiastic people. Enthusiasm, like all attitudes, is contagious. We prefer to be around people who are enthusiastic.

You can only develop enthusiasm through positive attitudes. Enthusiasm comes from an attitude of mind. The word enthusiasm comes from a Greek word, entheos, which, when translated, means "possessed by God." Maybe that's why it is such a powerful attitude!

THE BENEFITS OF ENTHUSIASM

Personally, I want to live enthusiastically. I would hate for my family to read my obituary someday and find out that "on his last day he was miserable." Since I don't know when my last day will be, I have to strive to be enthusiastic every day.

Will Rogers told us that it only takes three things to live life enthusiastically: **"Know what you're doing, love what you're doing, and believe in what you're doing."** When you do, you will live fully and successfully each day. Every day is important! Just try to miss one and you'll find out.

There is considerable evidence that enthusiasm and optimism will lengthen your life. The late John D. Rockefeller lived to be ninety-seven. With his enthusiasm, he wasn't ready to leave even then; they had to nail the coffin shut!

J. C. Penney was quoted as saying, "You can take all the money I have, all my stores, all my employees, even my health, but leave me my enthusiasm and I'll have it all again!" He did, in fact, experience such setbacks. Yet, enthusiasm kept him going and each time he came back greater than before.

BEGIN WITH A SMILE

The first step in developing enthusiasm is to learn to smile more. Smile **for** people, not **at them**. "So what's new? I've heard that before," you say. Yes, but you need to hear it again. Millions of words have been written extolling the virtues of a cheerful smile, yet if you sit at a busy airport, go shopping in a mall, eat in a restaurant or observe employees in the office, you'll notice that very few people are smiling. That's why we need to be reminded. We don't do enough of it.

Many people smile only when they are trying to impress someone. One survey observed that twelve percent of the time, men smile when they pass other men, but they smiled at seventy percent of the women. Were they saying that they cared more what women thought of them than what other men thought?

Smiling has a positive impact on those around us and it's also good for us. Some retail stores found sales increasing dramatically when they insisted their sales clerks smile more. A smile is a non-verbal form of communication. When we encounter another human being, isn't it a more positive experience if we're both smiling?

Ella Wheeler Wilcox, the poet, in her poem, "Worthwhile," says:

> 'Tis easy enough to be pleasant
> when life flows along like a song;
> But the man worthwhile is the one who will smile
> When everything goes dead wrong.

No one is suggesting that life will be all peaches and cream, but why not face it with a smile? A pleasant disposition and a smile are the most inexpensive gifts you can give another human being.

If you need proof of its value, practice smiling. Go into a room

87

alone tonight and sit in a chair. Consciously begin to smile and notice the relaxing feeling that comes over you. You can tell you were born to smile, and smiling is the beginning of establishing the habit of being enthusiastic.

Ralph Waldo Emerson said, "Nothing great was ever achieved without enthusiasm." Charles Schwab, chairman of the board of Bethlehem Steel, said, "A person can succeed at anything for which there is **enthusiasm**." Papyrus said, "No one keeps up his enthusiasm automatically." Enthusiasm must be nourished, practiced and applied over and over again. William James, the great Harvard psychologist, said it this way, "You feel the way you act. Act tired, you will feel tired. Act excited, you will feel excited."

STEPS TO DEVELOP ENTHUSIASM

In summary, let's look at some ways to develop enthusiasm and keep it going.

1. The first and most important step in developing enthusiasm is to remember this guideline: **to be enthusiastic you have to act enthusiastically.** Now when you get up in the morning, instead of just rolling over in bed, moaning and groaning, "Well, I suppose I'll have to get up and face this new day," leap out of bed. Jump out of that bed. You might even want to pound yourself on the chest a couple of times and say, "This is the day that the Lord hath made." What a way to start the day! What a way to develop some enthusiasm! Thinking good thoughts is important but action is what puts it into being, into reality. To be enthusiastic, you have to act enthusiastically.

2. **As much as possible, avoid people who are gloomy.** You know there are people all over who are preaching

doom and gloom and negativism and how the world doesn't seem to fit together. These people let problems and their external circumstances dictate the way they feel. They don't see anything to be happy about...and their unhappiness is as contagious as enthusiasm is. I saw a bumper sticker once that made a major impact on me (so much so, I used it as the title of this book). It said, "Attitudes are contagious...are yours worth catching?" I liked the bumper stick because I had discovered that negative attitudes are just as "catching" as positive ones. So beware of people who preach doom and gloom, because you can catch those feelings just like you can catch enthusiasm. You've got to avoid the habitual reinforcement of those negative attitudes.

3. **Have a healthy attitude toward problems.** Of course, those of us who are enthusiastic are not immune from problems. Just remember, though, it is the way in which we look at them that creates the problems. If we have a healthy attitude toward problems, we realize that problems are the best friends we have. If we don't have a problem we don't have a purpose for living. You need to realize that if you've got five, good, old-fashioned, king-size problems and another individual has ten, that individual is probably twice as alive as you are. Problems are a sign of life. So take a healthy approach to problems.

    Solve annoying little problems or dismiss them entirely. Holding on to them blocks out the important things. Get rid of routine and monotonous chores the first thing each day. Never stop learning. The broader one's knowledge, the more enthusiasm will be generated. Block out other problems in your life or enthusiasm will suffer immediately.

4. **Realize that every adversity can be an opportunity.** An old saying that "adversity is just opportunity in wolf's clothing" is a good way of putting it. But we have to recognize and realize that we can turn our adversities into opportunities if we have a healthy, enthusiastic attitude. A healthy, enthusiastic attitude! You can read article after article which detail how people only find the greatness in themselves when they are faced with the most difficult times of their lives. Sometimes it's hard to get up and look past an adversity that's knocked you down and realize that this adversity is really good for you.

   How can you feel good about getting knocked down? Perhaps you can't feel good about it, but you'll keep on "keeping on." Remember, Vince Lombardi said, "It doesn't matter how many times you get knocked down, it's how many times you get up." Learn something from the fall. And if every time you get up you're a better person than when you were knocked down, you'll turn adversity into opportunity.

5. **When something is done, forget it**. We spend more than eighty percent of our time worrying about things we can't do anything about. When a job is done, forget it. Do your best when you are doing a job and then don't worry about it. The world is full of people who worry and fret and are in a total shambles because they second-guess their own decisions. And you find some people who put off making a decision for fear of making the wrong decision.

I truly believe that it is sometimes better to make the wrong decision than to make no decision at all. Accept that as an important part of enthusiasm: When the job is done, forget it. Former president Harry Truman is a good example of a person who could do that. Truman always said the day he made the decision to drop the atomic bombs he went to bed and slept well because it was too late to do anything about it; the planes were already on their way. That's a healthy attitude toward decision making. The job is done, forget it. There is nothing more that can be done about it.

6.   **Keep everything in perspective.** Try to recognize that those things that got you down today won't even be remembered next week. Put it all in perspective. How important is this thing that you're worrying about? How important is it, really? Probably not too important in the whole scheme of things. Often times we laugh about a thing after it is over, but at the moment we are going through it, it certainly isn't very funny. If you are going to laugh later, why not laugh now, and reduce the amount of stress you place on yourself? Keep your day's activities in perspective...it keeps you from wasting energy on things you can't really do anything about.

7.   **Look for new goals.** Life is an exciting journey if you have goals. New goals contain exciting and unexpected elements which are always an aid to building enthusiasm. Goals give us a purpose and direction in life. It's easier to be enthusiastic when we know where we're going. Goal setting is so important that it's an entire chapter in itself!

8.   **Be confident.** Enthusiasm stays alive on small attainments

91

as well as major ones. Slow down that constant comparison to how others are doing in their efforts. This will help keep enthusiasm alive. The only person you're in competition with is the person you see in the mirror every morning.

9. **Watch your health.** Poor health can cause depression. It is important to take care of your body as well as your mind — the two must exist in harmony. It is important each day to spend a little time in complete relaxation. One's mind needs rest periods in order to keep generating enthusiasm.

10. **Smile.** Sincerely learn to smile. No one needs a smile as badly as a person who doesn't have one to give you. So give them freely and recognize that it takes only half as much energy to smile as it does to frown. Did you ever notice that people who frown a lot always look tired? That's why! They're burning up all that energy — they are tired! They need to learn to smile so they have more energy, more "get up and go."

If you really feel you need to frown, set aside a frowning time from 8 to 9 o'clock each night. In so doing, you'll save your strength all day. You can't be wasting energy all day frowning; you've got to save up energy so you can put on a real king-size from tonight at 8 o'clock. You know what will happen? When 8 p.m. comes you won't have anything to frown about! As you practice and practice the habit of smiling, it becomes easier and easier to do. A good habit is as easy to develop as a poor one. Now isn't that true?

From now on if somebody says, "How are you doing?"

say, "Super, but I'll be better tomorrow." That's enthusiasm you can generate on your own! At work, how about coming in on Monday and saying, "Thank God it's Monday! It's great to be back!"

ENTHUSIASM IS CONTAGIOUS — START AN EPIDEMIC TODAY!

THE VALUE OF A SMILE

It costs nothing, but creates much.

It enriches those who receive without impoverishing those who give.

It happens in a flash, and the memory of it sometimes lasts forever.

None are so rich they can get along without it, and none so poor but are richer for its benefits.

It creates happiness in the home, fosters goodwill in a business, and is the countersign of friends.

It is rest to the weary, daylight to the discouraged, sunshine to the sad, and nature's best antidote for trouble.

Yet it cannot be bought, begged, borrowed, or stolen, for it is something that is no earthly good to anyone until it is given away.

And if in the course of the day some of your friends should be too tired to give you a smile, why don't you give them one of yours?

For nobody needs a smile so much as those who have none left to give!

SMILE!

—ANONYMOUS

I'd like to close this chapter with a remarkable story told by the late Norman Vincent Peale in one of his sermons:

"Recently, there were two items in the newspaper on the same page. One was about a girl, twenty-one years old, the other about a man eighty-one years old. Sadly, his 'satanic majesty' had certainly got in his licks with the twenty-one-year-old girl. But the eighty-one-year-old man managed to hold him off with vibrant enthusiasm.

"Here was a note left by the girl who had committed suicide:

> 'I am twenty-one. I have seen everything. I know everything. I don't like life. It's cheap, dirty, disappointing. I've had all I want of it.'

"That was it. Then she put a bullet through her head. Victim of a rotting, sophisticated society in which the poor little thing lost her way and finally gave up due to cynicism and depression.

"Here's what the man of eighty-one said:

> 'I haven't lived long enough. I have only seen a few of the amazing wonders of this world. There are so many things that I don't know and that I want to know. I have enjoyed every minute of this life. I would like to live every day of it over again.'

"End of quote. No bullet to the brain. The difference between these two people-separated by many years and by even greater wisdom-is the faith and enthusiasm for life that the old man had."

It's a choice each of us makes each day. How will you choose to see tomorrow? It is up to you.

EPILOGUE

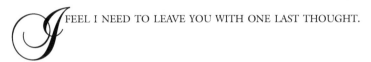 FEEL I NEED TO LEAVE YOU WITH ONE LAST THOUGHT.

If you have decided there is something you are going to change or do as a result of reading this book, begin now. Don't wait another moment. If something is going to enrich your life or improve your relationships with people, isn't it important enough to start doing NOW?

The story I'm about to share with you will illustrate what I mean.

One of the programs my company offers is called "Adventures In Attitudes." Within that program are ten sessions dealing with various aspects of personal improvement. Normally, we offer the program in a ten-week format, meeting one night a week for ten weeks.

During one particular session a very significant event occurred. I was teaching a class for fourteen women and six men on Tuesday nights. On the second Tuesday of our sessions I did the "unpardonable." I gave the class homework! (Adults dislike homework even more than kids.) The assignment was to go to someone you love within the next week and tell them you love them. It was to be someone they had never said those words to before or at least hadn't shared that feeling with for a long time. Now that doesn't sound like a very tough assignment until you stop to realize that most of the men in that group were over 35 and were raised in the generation of men that were taught that expressing emotions is not "macho." Showing feelings or crying (heaven forbid!) was just not done. So this ended up being a very threatening assignment for some.

At the beginning of our next class, I asked if someone wanted to share what happened when they told someone they loved them. I fully expected one of the women to volunteer, as was usually the case, but on this evening one of the men raised his hand volunteering to share what had happened to him. He appeared quite moved and a bit shaken.

As he unfolded out of his chair (all 6'2" of him), he began by saying, "Dennis, I was quite angry with you last week when you gave us this assignment. I didn't feel that I had anyone to say those words to, and besides, who were you to tell me to do something that personal? But as I began driving home, my conscience started talking to me. It was telling me that I knew **exactly** who I needed to say "I love you" to. You see five years ago, my father and I had a vicious disagreement and really never resolved it since that time. We avoided seeing each other unless we absolutely had to at Christmas or other family gatherings. But even then, we hardly spoke to each other. So, last Tuesday by the time I got home I had convinced myself I was going to tell my father I loved him.

"It's weird but just making that decision seemed to lift a heavy load off my chest.

"When I got home, I rushed into the house to tell my wife

what I was going to do. She was already in bed, but I woke her up anyway. When I told her, she didn't just get out of bed, she parachuted out and hugged me, and for the first time in our married life she saw me cry. We stayed up half the night drinking coffee and talking. It was great!

"The next morning I was up bright and early. I was so excited I could hardly sleep. I got to the office early and accomplished more in two hours than I had the whole day before." (Was this guy motivated or what?)

"At 9:00 I called my Dad to see if I could come over after work. When he answered, I just said, 'Dad, can I come over after work tonight? I have something to tell you.' My dad responded with a grumpy, 'Now what?' I assured him it wouldn't take long, so he finally agreed.

"At five-thirty, I was at my parents' house ringing the doorbell, praying that Dad would answer the door. I was afraid if Mom answered I would chicken out and tell her instead. But as luck would have it, Dad did answer the door. (Luck is opportunity meeting preparedness!)

"I didn't waste any time — I took one step in the door and said, 'Dad, I just came over to tell you that I love you.'

"It was as if a transformation came over my dad. Before my eyes his face softened, the wrinkles seemed to disappear and he began to cry. He reached out and hugged me and said, 'I love you too, son, but I've never been able to say it.'

"It was such a precious moment I didn't want to move. Mom walked by with tears in her eyes. I just waved and blew her a kiss. Dad and I hugged for a moment longer and then I left. I hadn't felt that great in a long time.

"But that's not even my point. Two days after that visit, my dad, who had heart problems but didn't tell me, had an attack and ended up in the hospital, unconscious. I don't know if he'll make it.

"So my message to all of you in this class is this. Don't wait to do the things you know need to be done. What if I had waited to tell my dad — maybe I will never get the chance again! Take the time to do what you need to do and **DO IT NOW!**"

This story is so moving I use it to end many of my speeches, and so I feel it is appropriate to end my book in the same way.

Take heed of the message of this one man's story. Maybe you'll have a similar one to tell. Many have come to me with the same kind of story, some with happy endings, and some, very tragic.

So, I urge you, whatever you feel you need to do — whether it's telling someone you care, setting those goals, striving to be more positive, becoming more enthusiastic, learning to listen better, spending more time with your loved ones — **don't wait!** Find a way to do it **and** DO IT NOW!

POSTSCRIPT
FROM DENNIS MANNERING

THANKS TO YOU, THE READER. THIS IS A BOOK WRITten for you with the hope that you will not just purchase it, but read it. One recent statistic tells us that thirty-seven percent of the population will never read a book after they leave high school. What a shame!

If I've made a difference for you, no matter how great or how small, I am grateful. The greatest contribution we can make to another person is to help them grow. But don't stop here. Keep growing and learning. The world is waiting for each of us to make that same contribution to another. It is what life is all about!

ABOUT THE AUTHOR

ENNIS MANNERING WAS BORN ON JANUARY 23, 1942 and grew up in the foothills of the Ozark Mountains in southwestern Missouri.

He is the sixth of seven children and was raised mainly by his mother, since his father deserted the family when he was five. Around the same time his father left, Dennis had a bad case of scarlet fever which is believed to have been the cause of a severe hearing loss. With the type of loss Dennis had, a hearing aid was not recommended. Only since 1983 has new technology provided a hearing aid that would help.

When he was fourteen, his mother realized she was unable to support all her children. Dennis was sent to upstate New York to live with his brother. He graduated from high school in Cato, New York.

While attending college at Southwest Missouri State in Springfield, MO he noticed that he was losing weight, but attributed it to a busy schedule. He was working nights full time and going to school by day.

When he was recruited to teach in the inner city of Milwaukee and took his required physical, he was told he could not teach because he had active signs of tuberculosis. By this time, Dennis had two children and a wife to support, so this was not good news. By some miracle, when he went back to get re-tested three weeks later, his lung scars were considered healed enough that he could teach. He was never treated in any way for tuberculosis (except for the fervent prayers of his mother and family).

He had six rewarding years teaching in the inner city of Milwaukee where he related well to the students due to his southern upbringing and understanding of that culture. He taught sales and marketing at the high school level. During this time his third child was born, but Dennis continued to work on his education, earning his Masters degree in the summers from the University of Wisconsin-Madison.

Though his early life was full of adversity, Dennis never saw it that way. He saw his life as full and challenging and did what he had to do to survive. He often says now, "I never knew I lived in a dysfunctional family. I never realized I was poor. I didn't realize I had a disability. Nobody ever told me I had all these excuses to fail, so I just kept on trying to achieve, and with the help of God and a lot of wonderful people, I am where I am today."

To date, Dennis has earned a Masters degree, has received the Speaking Star award from his Wisconsin chapter of the National Speakers Association and earned the Certified Speaking Professional (CSP) designation from the National Speakers Association. He has written three books, produced four video learning systems and five audiocassette albums and has traveled as far as the Pacific Rim to do seminars.

As a volunteer he serves as an elder for his church, mentors with young people going through their confirmation of faith, is active in his community business organizations and has received the Outstanding Service Award for his years of service and dedication to marketing education in Wisconsin.

He has three adult sons of which he is very proud and has the love and adoration of five wonderful grandchildren. He and his wife work together in their business, traveling and speaking.

Comments Welcome

*I*F YOU WOULD LIKE TO COMMENT REGARDING THIS book, call or write Dennis E. Mannering or Wendy K. Mannering at the address below:

Options Unlimited, Inc.
617 Sunrise Lane
Green Bay, WI 54301
920-339-0011 Fax 920-339-0012
Email Dmannering@aol.com or Wmannering@aol.com
Website http://members.aol.com/Mannerings

If you would like information regarding Dennis or Wendy's speaking and seminar services, you may also reach them at the above address and telephone number.

ORDER INFORMATION

Other products available through Options Unlimited, Inc.

Audio Cassette Albums
Motivation in Action (Dennis Mannering)
Selling Your Way to Success (Dennis Mannering)
Attitudes Are Contagious...Are Yours Worth Catching? (Dennis Mannering)
How Good Managers Become Great Leaders (Dennis Mannering)
Do They Know They're on Your Team? (Wendy Mannering)

Books by Dennis Mannering
How Good Managers Become Great Leaders
Everyday Heroes
The Winning Spirit (An anthology)

Videos by Dennis Mannering
Astounding Your Customers With Service
Building the Ultimate Customer Service Team
Selling Your Way to Success

Attitudes Are Contagious...Are Yours Worth Catching? T-Shirts and Mugs
Live a 7/7th Life T-Shirt

Newsletter
The Mannering Report (Published six times per year)

To order call: 1-800-236-3445
or fax your order to 920-339-0012